the perfectly
tossed

MINDY FOX

the perfectly tossed salad

FRESH, DELICIOUS AND ENDLESSLY VERSATILE

PHOTOGRAPHY BY ELLEN SILVERMAN
KYLE BOOKS

First published in Great Britain in 2012 by
Kyle Books
23 Howland Street
London
W1T 4AY
general.enquiries@kylebooks.com
www.kylebooks.com

ISBN: 978-0-85783-042-5

Text © 2012 by Mindy Fox
Photographs © 2012 by Ellen Silverman
Book design © 2012 by Kyle Books

Project editor Anja Schmidt
Designer Carl Hodson
Photographer Ellen Silverman
Food styling Rebecca Jurkevich
Prop styling Lucy Attwater
Copy editor Sarah Scheffel
Production Gemma John and Nic Jones

A cataloguing in Publication record for this
title is available from the British Library.

Colour reproduction by Scanhouse
Printed and bound in China by Toppan Leefung

introduction

I have always loved salad. My understanding of exactly what a 'salad' is, though, has dramatically evolved as my life has progressed.

I grew up in the 1970s and spent the better part of my pre-teen years in the Chicago suburbs. It was the dawn of the gourmet food shop, but most people still shopped at supermarkets, where the lettuce section consisted of orbs of iceberg and random heads of romaine – nothing like the luxurious line-up of salad leaves we enjoy today.

My mother was brilliant in the kitchen – an original food enthusiast. She showed my brother Jason and I how to fry prawn crackers, lovingly lacquer spare ribs with home-made barbecue sauce and pinch out basil leaves from her small back-garden herb patch, opening our eyes to the magic of kitchen alchemy and garden-to-table eating. Still, in keeping with the times, her vegetables during those years were purchased at the supermarket, and mostly they were cooked on the hob or in the fondue pot.

The raw vegetables I encountered in my early life were on the crudités plate at my grandmother's beach house. Nanny never missed her ritual five o'clock vodka, and with it she offered a glass platter of perfectly chilled, impossibly crisp veggies: crunchy radishes, those peppery and pretty red baubles with icy white insides that excited my taste buds; cucumber spears, their thick skins peeled away but sweet seeds left intact; freshly sliced celery with pleasingly bitter juices that tickled my tongue; and bright, snappy carrot-stick soldiers.

When I was a teenager my family decamped to New England. Mom's little herb patch was replaced by a rural expanse filled with apple trees. Her new gardens yielded rhubarb in the early spring, and raspberries and blueberries that popped from their buds as the weather grew warmer. In the summer, nasturtiums and courgette flowers spilled over flagstone walls. Our new way of life dovetailed nicely with Mom's ever-evolving flair for food and cooking. Her gorgeous green salads, lightly tossed with home-made garlic and fresh herb dressing, filled a well-seasoned wooden bowl nightly. Salads came alive for me then.

In college I spent a year in Paris studying film and photography. I lived on my own in a seventh-floor apartment on the Right Bank. My tiny garret dwelling consisted of twin beds, a small armoire, tiny wash basin and single-burner hotplate. I went to the market daily, *comme les Parisiennes*, since it was de rigueur and because I didn't have a fridge. Jean-François, my first French friend, shared my passion for cooking and taught me how to make *salade d'endives*. He cut the spear-shaped chicory crossways into thick, crunchy slices and seasoned it simply, with olive oil, a touch of vinegar and good salt. The occasional variation included a sprinkling of toasted walnuts and/or a crumble of creamy Roquefort cheese. Preparing no-fuss elemental salads such as this, born of necessity and driven by local and seasonal ingredients, quickly became cherished habit.

My fondness for food became my *métier*. Along with it came other significant salad discoveries: my friend, Sara Jenkins, a talented professional chef, taught me to make fattouche, sharing the brilliant Lebanese technique of mashing garlic with salt then stirring in fresh lemon juice for a rich, citrusy dressing without the harsh garlic bite. Watching Italian chef Matteo Boglione prepare his delicious salad of cheese, farro, artichoke and pecorino Toscano in the test kitchen of *La Cucina Italiana* magazine, I learned the joy of a thinly shaved, uncooked artichoke. A lifetime of adventurous eating and nearly two decades as a chef, food editor and writer, and yet I had never eaten a raw artichoke! I love that there is always something new to learn about cooking and eating.

Today, my answer to that impossible question: which one dish would I take to a desert island? A salad. There's no other dish I crave as often, regardless of the season. I continue to be inspired to prepare and eat extraordinary salads every day, a pleasure I'm delighted to share with you.

Vegetarians, vegans and meat-eaters can all enjoy this book as the recipes can be made without cheese, fish, meat and nuts. Also many of the dressings can be used independently, so non-dairy options can be substituted. I hope this book brings much joy to your salad-making kitchen and that you'll visit me at mindyfox.net to share your salad and other eating adventures or check out mine.

why a whole book on salad?

In my hectic and hurried everyday life, I've become adept at throwing together what I call 'elemental salads'. These few-ingredient salads are often unplanned. I open the fridge and make do with what's there: usually a few offerings that reflect the season. In winter, a lone bulb of fennel, perhaps, with its pretty fronds attached. I thinly shave the bulb, dress it with a healthy drizzle of good olive oil, a grating of lemon zest and a generous squeeze of juice, then sprinkle it with good salt, coarse black pepper and those delicate fronds. Served with a wedge of nice cheese, some grilled bread and a bowlful of olives, my husband Steve and I routinely call this dinner.

Our improvised salads often become favourites, later served to friends and family who delight in their simplicity. 'The same can be done with a head of celery!' I hear myself say, instructing them to thinly slice the stalks and save those beautiful leaves from the inner heart for sprinkling. 'If you happen on an apple, slice that too. Maybe add a few shavings of Parmigiano-Reggiano and a sprinkle of currants and toasted nuts…' and off I go on my well-worn riff about how to cobble together a super-satisfying weekday salad from a few arbitrary fridge and store cupboard bits.

I've always had a natural inclination towards eating healthy foods, but good health is not primarily what inspires me to make salads nor excites me about eating them. Instead it's the seemingly endless possibilities of what the dish can be – everything from a stunningly satisfying and gorgeous plate of raw vegetables dressed with good oil and sea salt to a more complex dish involving ingredients such as fruits, grains, cheese, eggs, fish, meat and more.

Salad is an approachable and appropriate dish at any time of the year. It fits both everyday and lavish occasions, provides punch to a meal of many courses, or serves as a meal on its own. Great salads invite you to dispose of those admonishing health-watch do-and-don't lists and simply enjoy the pleasure of cooking and eating beautiful, healthy, vibrant seasonal food.

thinking beyond greens

Salad often infers a bowl of greens, and a bowl of good greens is indeed delicious. But beyond that bowl, a salad can be so much more. Here's a brief primer on a broader range of salad components.

VEGETABLES AND FRUITS in salads can be all raw, all cooked or a mix of both. Before you start to slice, consider the characteristics of your ingredients. A thinly shaved fennel bulb offers a delicate flavour and texture, but if cut thickly its anise flavour is more robust. Pickled vegetables and fruits (like carrots or peaches) make great salad ingredients; they can be shop-bought or quickly prepared at home. (Note: Quick pickles are not preserved, so they should be eaten within a week or so.) Dried fruits, such as cranberries and raisins, offer pleasing rich- or tart-sweet notes.

GRAINS, LEGUMES AND BEANS bring exceptional nutritional depth to salads, as well as great flavour and texture. These ingredients can play the lead role (a white bean or lentil salad, for example) or be used as an accent in green salads.

NUTS AND SEEDS lend texture, earthy flavour and good fats to a salad. Good fats are monounsaturated and polyunsaturated fats. They're found in high concentrations in nuts, seeds, and nut and seed oils.

EGGS, PASTA AND POTATOES are the stalwarts of the salad world. They're also crowd-pleasers and travel well to bring-and-share suppers, picnics and beach outings. I've taken a new look at these classics in this book.

FRESH HERBS are among my favourite salad ingredients. I use them liberally, chopped and folded into dressings, sprinkled over the top or incorporated as whole leaves.

CHEESES OF ALL SORTS — soft, hard, young, aged, mild and/or robust — are delicious and tend to work fantastically in both planned and impromptu salads.

SALT AND SALTY INGREDIENTS like olives, capers and anchovies sometimes announce themselves but often they are used as subtle flavour enhancers.

my seven secrets to extraordinary salads

Like every facet of cooking, making a really good salad involves a little craft and basic know-how. Here are my top seven salad-making tips:

1. **SOURCE IMPECCABLY:** All good cooking begins with good shopping. This does not necessarily mean breaking the bank: a great salad can be made with just a handful of ingredients, and inexpensive ones at that. What it does mean is choosing your ingredients with care and remaining flexible enough to work with the best of what's available. Purchasing seasonal ingredients at a farmers' market or good-quality food market is ideal – the produce is most often picked the day you buy, and the animal proteins on offer are usually among the healthiest options available. But knowing that you can make a fantastic salad from a few bulbs of quality fennel or a head of sturdy, fresh celery – common all year round, even at most groceries – is a great relief when you don't feel like fussing in the kitchen or need to put together an easy, quick dish with ingredients you already have on hand.

Choosing the best of what's available is more important than sticking rigidly to a recipe. Sometimes this means straying from the main route, but with an understanding of basic ingredients it's easy to take good detours. Salad greens, for example, tend to fall into three flavour categories: sweet (including Bibb or red- and green-leaf lettuces), bitter (radicchio, chicory, frisée and escarole, for example) and peppery (rocket, baby mustard and watercress among them). Most varieties within a flavour category can stand in for one another quite well. Ingredient swaps are not limited to greens. Try a crisp, sweet-tart apple in place of a pear, for example, or stoned fresh cherries or a sliced nectarine in lieu of sectioned blood oranges. Each time you stray from or play with a recipe, whether out of necessity or whimsy, your cooking prowess and confidence grows. (For ingredient resources and helpful books on how to choose and prepare fruits and vegetables, see Sources, page 170.)

2. **PREPARE GREENS WITH CARE:** Washing, drying, tearing and handling greens gently will help prevent wilting and keep them bright and unblemished for best flavour and good looks. Use a sharp paring knife to trim just the base of head lettuces, then separate the leaves. Fill a large bowl (or, for very big batches of greens, a clean sink) with very cold water (the temperature is important as cold water will help perk up greens; add a few ice cubes, if necessary), submerge the leaves, then gently agitate with your hands. Leave the greens to sit undisturbed for 5–10 minutes, during which time dirt and grit will sink to the bottom, then, without agitating so that the grit stays underneath, lift the greens out of the water. If greens are particularly dirty, repeat once or twice with a rinsed bowl or sink and fresh water.

Dry greens in small batches in a salad spinner, then, if you have time, carefully spread them out on a clean, dry tea towel and cover (without pressing) with a second lightweight towel or kitchen paper to dry more completely. Dressing coats thoroughly dry greens best.

It's generally best to tear large leaves and tender herbs, like basil, by hand rather than chopping them, to prevent bruising, though rinsed and dried basil leaves can also be cut into a chiffonade or thinly sliced.

3. **BE SALT (AND PEPPER) SAVVY:** A high-quality salt is arguably the single most important ingredient in your kitchen. It pulls forth the flavours of a dish while adding its own characteristic sparkle to both raw and cooked foods. Depending on which type you use, salt also contributes flavour notes of mineral, brine, sweet, sharp, buttery, smoky, floral, fruity and more. Good salts are unprocessed, unrefined and additive-free.

My preferred cooking salt (the one that I use to flavour water for cooking pasta, rice, potatoes and blanched vegetables) is a basic unprocessed fine-grained sea salt. This can be found at most good supermarkets and can often be purchased in bulk. I do spend a bit more of my food budget on unprocessed salt than I would on a common table or kosher salt (the latter both include chemicals I prefer to avoid), but it is not a budget-breaker. For me, the health and flavour benefits outweigh a bit of added expense.

For seasoning and finishing (a last sprinkle, just before serving), or for a more distinctive taste or texture, I might use the same basic fine sea salt. I keep

maldon smoked
flake salt

fiore di sale
di trapani

balinese coarse
hollow pyramids

a variety of fine-grained, medium-grained and flaky coarse sea salts on hand. There are no rules as to which one to use when, just a few suggestions.

Fine-grained sea salts are perfect for salad dressings because they incorporate and dissolve well. Medium-grained and flaky sea salts are best for finishing a dish. A few examples of these salts include Maldon or Murray River (crunchy flake salts) and fleur de sel or fiore di sale (Italian fleur de sel). There are dozens of inspiring salts from around the world, and they're becoming more readily available as demand increases. As with wine or olive oil, the best way to become familiar with salts is to taste them.

An important distinction when seasoning is 'tasting the salt' in a dish (seasoning appropriately) as opposed to a dish 'tasting salty' (oversalting). You do want to taste a salt element in your food; that wonderfully briny, clean pop that makes other ingredients come alive. However, just at the point where you can taste salt and the flavours of the other ingredients in your dish brighten, you have seasoned well and enough. For best success, season gradually, tasting as you go.

A quick word on salt and health. Salt is not a 'bad' ingredient: we all actually need salt in our bodies to varying degrees. When you cook using high-quality unprocessed ingredients and season with good-tasting unprocessed salt, you're likely to use less salt; your food is being seasoned, not masked, by the salt. Most salt-related health problems do not come from using good-quality salt on unprocessed foods, but rather from eating processed and packaged foods that contain much higher amounts of sodium than one would use when seasoning unprocessed home-cooked foods. Per dietary requirements, adjust salt in recipes as needed.

When it comes to pepper, seasoning is a bit simpler: black, white and pink peppercorns (which are actually not peppercorns but dried berries) deliver their best flavour when freshly ground or crushed. A good-quality pepper mill will allow you to vary your grind from coarse to fine and is a worthwhile investment. The size of your grind (coarse or fine) is as much a matter of preference as anything else. For a large, coarse crush, use a small, heavy-based frying pan, pressing down on the pan and gently rolling it over the peppercorns. (For salt and pepper suppliers, see Sources, page 170.)

4. LEARN HOW TO SELECT, STORE AND USE OIL AND VINEGAR: I cook primarily with extra virgin olive oil and generally keep three to four types on hand. The first is a good-quality basic extra virgin olive oil, which I use for cooking and in some salad dressings. This type of oil is widely available in most supermarkets and has very good basic flavour. To help keep oil-buying economical, I purchase 3-litre tins, transferring the oil (with the help of a mini plastic funnel) to a small, easy-to-grasp glass bottle. I use this basic oil to cook with and in my more complex salad dressings (those with strong-flavoured ingredients, where the nuances of a premium extra virgin olive oil would be lost).

Heating olive oil does not ruin or rob it of its flavour, but it will diminish the finer characteristics of higher-priced, estate-bottled extra virgin olive oils. These types of oils are referred to as 'finishing oils', because they are most appropriate for drizzling on a dish just before serving. I use these oils in delicately flavoured dressings and to drizzle over elemental salads, like those in chapter one of this book.

Finishing oils and speciality vinegars are often marked with the name of an estate, a vintage and/or a 'use by' date on the label, bottle or bottleneck. Fine olive oils come from Italy, Spain, France, Greece, Morroco, South Africa, New Zealand, California, Chile and beyond. They range in flavour from piquant to mellow (with many variations in between) and in colour from green to gold. The best way to find oils and vinegars that you love is to buy and taste.

Having two or three finer oils, each with different characteristics – one might be peppery, the other grassy or fruity – gives you options to play with. Since it's best to use up premium oils within a year from the time the olives were pressed, and within a few months after opening, I keep only a few oils on hand.

In addition to extra virgin olive oils, there are nut oils and light, neutral-tasting salad oils, like grapeseed. Nut oils and grapeseed oil are very sensitive and can rapidly go rancid after opening. Since I don't use up nut oils quickly, I find it easier to work with nuts than to keep the oils fresh. Heat and light are foes to all oils. When possible, choose oils packaged in tinted glass, and keep bottles stored in a cool, dark place. Store sensitive oils (and nuts too) in the fridge and use them up within a few months after opening.

There are myriad wonderful vinegars to choose from for salad-making. Having a good-quality red and white wine, balsamic and white balsamic, cider and aged sherry vinegar on hand will get you through most of the recipes in this book. When buying balsamic vinegars, avoid purchasing those with the words 'sugar' and 'caramel' in the ingredients. These are low-quality and not true balsamics. Wonderful speciality and small-batch vinegars, such as Vin Santo vinegar from Italy, are great to add to your basics. When buying speciality vinegars, look for those with a stamped lot number and/or 'best by' date (sometimes in fine print or on the back label or neck of the bottle). Store vinegars as you would oils.

5. DRESS FOR SUCCESS: When it comes to dressing salads, my two cardinal rules are avoid bottled dressings and don't overdress. Many of the great salad cultures (Greek, Lebanese, Turkish, Israeli and Italian) use a simple blend of good olive oil, natural acid (citrus or vinegar) and good salt or salty ingredients, such as anchovies or capers. A dressing of this nature can take as little as two minutes to make and is just as convenient, far healthier, more economical and worlds more vibrant-tasting than any commercial dressing you can buy. Most week nights, I season greens with fresh lemon juice or a good vinegar and

a drizzle of good olive oil. With a little more time, I'll soften and sweeten a tablespoon or two of finely chopped shallot or red onion in vinegar for 10–30 minutes, then whisk in oil and season with salt and pepper. A more complex dressing might involve fresh herbs, olives, garlic or crushed or ground dried chillies, such as Aleppo or piment d'Espelette. Dressings can go beyond the expected: a pesto can be thinned out with a touch of warm water or extra oil for easy tossing; classic sauces like Italian salsa verde, Turkish tarator and chimichurri make exciting salad dressings as well.

Some cookbooks suggest a 3:1 ratio of oil to acid for salad dressings. I prefer a more flexible approach. The perfect acid–oil balance can change per salad. For example, assertive salad greens, such as chicory, might demand a slightly heavier acid hand, whereas a delicate lettuce, like lamb's lettuce, almost always requires a softer touch. Some salads are best with oil only. Vinegar types may vary in acid intensity; personal preference varies as well. While 3:1 is a starting place, being open to variations when making your own dressings often works best. Taste as you can go.

To avoid overdressing, use a light coating of dressing on greens, nothing more. If you're unsure of how much to use, add in gradual increments.

6. MIX GENTLY, JUST A BIT AND IN A LARGE, WIDE BOWL: Not all salads are tossed, but for those that are, tossing is a critical step in the salad-making process. In just two to three gentle tosses, you want your dressing to lightly coat each ingredient, like fresh herbs or sprinklings of seeds. A large, wide bowl is the key to giving your ingredients the space they need to combine in just a few turns, and ensures greens won't bruise.

7. KNOW WHEN TO TOSS: Most rice, bean, potato, pasta and chicken salads improve in flavour when refrigerated for a day or two. But green salads, especially those with delicate or feathery leaves, quickly lose their vitality as they sit. All of your ingredients can be prepared ahead, but toss a green salad just before serving.

basic tools for extraordinary salads

These tools are my must-haves for salad-making. Fantastic investments, they are useful for other dishes as well.

BOWLS I use ceramic and wooden bowls for tossing and serving salad. The most important aspect in choosing a salad bowl is its size and shape. Use large, wide bowls (30–35cm, or larger, in diameter); the more people you are serving, the wider and deeper you want your bowl to be. To season a new wooden bowl, rub a small amount of vegetable oil into the grain on the inside of the bowl. Repeat every few days for two weeks, then once or twice a year. Avoid using soap to wash wooden bowls, which causes drying and cracking. Instead, rinse with very hot or boiling water, then towel- and air-dry completely before storing.

A set of measuring prep bowls, which allow you to measure out and prepare the various ingredients of your recipe, is invaluable for salads and other dishes. Preparing an entire ingredient list before tossing or cooking helps you cook better. You'll focus solely on the assembly or cooking rather than dashing back to your chopping board to cut or slice.

A 'rubbish bowl' – a medium bowl for discarding vegetable peels, outer lettuce leaves and other scraps as you prepare – makes you a quicker, more focused and neater cook as it means you don't have to walk back and forth from the chopping board to the bin.

SALTS On my kitchen worktop, I keep a sealed jar of unprocessed fine sea salt and another filled with a coarse flaky sea salt; these are the two I reach for daily. Additional speciality finishing salts are stored in sealed containers in my store cupboard. To serve salts at the table, use small bowls or ceramic dishes, returning salts to airtight containers after each meal to keep them moist and fresh. (See page 10 for more about salt.)

PEPPER MILL Pepper mills are like umbrellas – the cheap ones don't tend to work very well or for very long. The flavour of freshly ground pepper is certainly worth the investment of a good mill, and a good one should last a lifetime. I've had great luck with Peugeot mills, which cost between £25 and £50 and make a wonderful gift. (See Sources, page 170.)

MANDOLINE Also called an adjustable slicer or V-slicer, I use my mandoline to cut vegetables and firm fruits into matchstick-like strips, known as julienne (hard to do with a knife, especially when you want thin cross sections of round vegetables such as onions and radishes). You can purchase a quality plastic Japanese mandolin for around £30 (I've had the same plastic Benriner model for years) or spend more on a heavy-duty stainless steel sort. City dwellers will find many types in Chinese supermarkets, which are always fun to poke around in. (See Sources, page 170.)

SHARP KNIVES Every cookbook worth its salt specifies good knives, and for good reason. High-quality, well-cared-for knives make a significant impact on the way that you cook. Cutting with precision prevents bruising, which helps keep ingredients fresh. It also ensures that your knife won't slip, which helps prevent cuts. There are lots of great knives out there, each with its own characteristics. Weights and shapes of handles and blades vary, and the best one for you is one that's comfortable in your hand. Test out knives in shops and choose based on comfort. One 15–20cm chef's knife, one paring knife and a good bread knife will cover most home cooks' needs.

SALAD SPINNER This simple, inexpensive tool is widely available, comes in compact and standard sizes, and makes quick work of rinsing and drying salad greens and sturdy fresh herbs such as parsley. When I have time, I lay out spun greens on a clean tea towel for further drying.

CITRUS SQUEEZER This tool is great for getting every last drop of tangy lemon, lime, orange or grapefruit juice out of the fruit and into your salad dressing or juice glass. Sizes and models range from worktop versions (choose from electric and manual) to smaller hand-held devices.

chapter one:

fennel, olives and oranges

Well-chilled fruit and a good-quality citrus-pressed extra virgin olive oil are key elements here. Freeing the orange sections from their insulating thick skins and then chilling them boosts their flavour and juiciness. If you're pressed for time, chill the fruit for at least 10 minutes. If you can't find the citrus oil, use a good-quality, fruity extra virgin olive oil, plus a squeeze or two of fresh lemon or orange juice.

SERVES 4 TO 6

2 navel oranges
3 small heads of fennel,
  including stems and fronds
flaky coarse sea salt
65g Gaeta or Kalamata olives,
  stoned and halved
60ml blood orange, tangerine or
  clementine extra virgin olive
  oil (see Sources, page 170)

Using a sharp paring knife, trim off the tops and bottoms of the oranges. Stand 1 orange on its end and carefully cut the peel and pith from the flesh, following the curve of the fruit from the top to the bottom. Working over a large bowl, carefully cut each section away from the membranes and drop the sections into the bowl. Repeat with the remaining orange (the membranes can be snacked on or discarded). Chill the orange segments in a covered bowl or sealed container in the fridge for 2 hours or up to 1 day.

Cut the orange segments crossways into 3–4 pieces each.

Cut the stems and fronds from the fennel bulbs, then trim the bulbs. Cut the bulbs in half lengthways, then thinly slice. Coarsely chop enough of the fennel fronds to make 2–3 tablespoons.

Arrange the fennel pieces on a large serving platter or in a wide, shallow bowl. Crush several generous pinches of salt over the top of each layer, or just over the top if you have a single layer. Sprinkle the orange segments, olives and chopped fronds over the fennel, then drizzle the salad with the oil, and crush a few more generous pinches of salt over the top.

roasted parsnips, toasted hazelnuts and lamb's lettuce

Lamb's lettuce is tiny green, slightly nutty leaves. If you can't find it, there are lots of great stand-ins. Try torn radicchio leaves, baby rocket, watercress, mizuna or young dandelion greens – each pairs a little differently with the caramelised parsnips and sweet-tart balsamic syrup.

SERVES 4

450–600g parsnips, peeled and
   sliced lengthways
2 tablespoons extra virgin
   olive oil
flaky coarse sea salt
40g hazelnuts, finely chopped
2½ tablespoons good-quality
   balsamic vinegar
55g lamb's lettuce
2 teaspoons good-quality extra
   virgin olive oil for drizzling

Position a rack in the middle of the oven and preheat to 200°C/gas mark 6. Line a rimmed baking tray with baking paper.

Arrange the parsnips in a single layer on the baking tray, putting the smaller pieces in the centre (vegetables arranged closer to the edges of the tray will cook more quickly). Drizzle with the olive oil, then crush ¾ teaspoon of salt over the top. Roast for 15 minutes. Rotate the tray, turning over any parsnips that are golden on the bottom and moving darker pieces in towards the centre and lighter pieces out to the edges of the tray. Continue to roast for a further 10–12 minutes, until tender and golden.

Sprinkle the nuts over the parsnips and roast until the nuts are fragrant and lightly golden, about 3 minutes. Transfer the tray to a wire rack.

Put the vinegar in your smallest saucepan and, over a very low heat so that the vinegar reduces but does not burn, gently simmer until thickened and reduced by half, about 3 minutes (keep an eye on it as the reduction can happen very fast). Remove from the heat.

Put the lamb's lettuce in a large, shallow bowl, then arrange the parsnips and nuts on top, sprinkling them with any remaining oil and salt from the pan. Drizzle with the reduced vinegar, crush a few generous pinches of salt over the top and drizzle with the very good oil.

robiola and chicory with a chestnut honey vinaigrette

This crunchy, bitter-sweet salad is paired with a square of robiola due latte (also sold as robiola bosina), an intensely creamy cheese that offers subtle hints of mushroom and garlic with just a touch of mustiness. Try the salad as a starter, after a main course or as light meal on its own.

SERVES 4

1 medium red onion, peeled
  and cut lengthways into
  1cm wedges
2 tablespoons extra virgin
  olive oil
fine sea salt and freshly ground
  black pepper
115g robiola due latte, softened
  at room temperature for
  45 minutes – 3 hours
340g chicory, cut on a slight
  diagonal into 1cm slices

VINAIGRETTE
2½ tablespoons chestnut honey
  (see Sources, page 170)
2½ tablespoons good-quality
  extra virgin olive oil
2½ teaspoons red wine vinegar
freshly ground black pepper
  and fine sea salt

Position a rack in the middle of the oven and preheat to 200°C/gas mark 6. Line a rimmed baking tray with baking paper.

In a medium bowl, toss the onions with the oil, ¼ teaspoon of salt and a generous grinding of pepper. Spread the onions in a single layer in the centre of the baking tray. Use a rubber spatula to scrape any oil and salt left in the bowl over the onions. Roast for 20–22 minutes, rotating halfway through, until the onions are tender with crisped edges. Transfer the onions on the baking paper to a wire rack and leave to cool for 10 minutes.

Now make the vinaigrette. In a large bowl, combine the honey, oil, vinegar, 1 teaspoon of warm water, several generous grindings of pepper and ⅛ teaspoon of salt. Whisk together well. Add the cooled onions, chicory, ½ teaspoon of salt and another generous grinding of pepper. Gently but thoroughly toss together.

Cut the cheese into 4 pieces and put each piece on a serving plate. Spoon mounds of the salad alongside the cheese. Drizzle with any dressing left in the bowl.

substitute strategy:

The chestnut honey, with its deep, earthy, slightly bitter notes, is a key component to this dish. Buckwheat honey makes a great stand-in, if you need a substitute. Most other honey varieties are too sweet to use here, so track down the chestnut or buckwheat, which is wonderful and certainly worth the effort. Robiola is sold in 8-ounce squares, but you only need 4 ounces here. That said, the cheese keeps beautifully and can also be enjoyed on its own or spread onto slices of a good baguette or crisp mild-tasting crackers. If Robiola is unavailable, try a ripe Brie or Camembert, instead. Whichever you use, the cheese is best when it has had a chance to come to room temperature, so remember to take it out of the fridge at least 45 minutes, or preferably 2 to 3 hours, before serving.

sweet oranges, celery leaves and smoked almonds

I love this salad as much for its minimalism as for its distinct notes of sweet, salty and smoky, plus a touch of pleasing bitterness from the tender celery leaves. Valencia oranges are a good type to use here.

SERVES 4

3 sweet navel or blood oranges (see Box)
1 celery heart (4–5 stalks and the leaves)
1 tablespoon fresh lemon juice
fine sea salt and freshly ground black pepper
2 tablespoons good-quality extra virgin olive oil
40g smoked almonds, coarsely chopped
flaky coarse sea salt

Using a sharp paring knife, trim off the tops and bottoms of the oranges. Stand 1 orange on its end and carefully cut the peel and pith from the flesh, following the curve of the fruit from the top to the bottom. Cut each section away from the membranes, and place in a large bowl. Squeeze the juices from the membranes into a second bowl. Repeat with the remaining oranges.

Trim the base of the celery heart; separate and rinse and dry the stalks, then pinch off and reserve the leaves. Thinly slice the stalks on a slight diagonal.

Add the sliced celery stalks and the leaves to the bowl with the orange sections, then add 3 tablespoons of the squeezed orange juice, the lemon juice, ¼ teaspoon of fine sea salt and a generous grinding of pepper.

Transfer the salad to a serving platter or wide, shallow bowl. Drizzle with the oil, then sprinkle with the nuts. Crush a few generous pinches of flaky coarse sea salt over the top.

blood oranges:

Since blood oranges are more tart than sweet, and their tartness can vary, use less of (or omit) the lemon juice. Blood orange size varies, too. Use four to five, if they are smaller than the average juice orange, three if they're about the same size or larger.

roasted beet and blood orange pico de gallo

The versatility of this salad perfectly captures the spirit of this chapter – I've tucked it into fish tacos, generously spooned it over double-thick pork chops and served it with cocktails as part of a meze. The beets and oranges for this dish are cut into fork-sized pieces, which I like, even for tacos, but they can also be chopped into smaller pieces, as for classic salsa.

SERVES 4 TO 6

4 medium beetroot (about
   450g), trimmed
3 medium blood oranges
45g very thinly sliced red onion
1 small hot chilli, very thinly
   sliced crossways
1 tablespoon good-quality
   extra virgin olive oil
1 teaspoon red wine vinegar
fine sea salt
2 tablespoons thinly sliced
   coriander leaves
flaky coarse sea salt

Position a rack in the middle of the oven and preheat to 200°C/gas mark 6.

Put the beets in a baking dish and add enough water to come about 1cm up the sides of the dish. Cover the dish tightly with foil and roast the beets for 45 minutes – 1 hour or more, depending on the size of the beets, until tender when pierced with a knife. Uncover and leave the beets to stand until cool enough to peel.

Meanwhile, using a sharp paring knife, trim off the tops and bottoms of the oranges. Stand 1 orange on its end and carefully cut the peel and pith from the flesh, following the curve of the fruit from the top to the bottom. Working over a large bowl, carefully cut each section away from the membranes and drop the sections into the bowl. Repeat with the remaining orange (the membranes can be snacked on or discarded).

Peel and cut the beets into 1cm-wide wedges, then transfer to the bowl with the orange sections and juice. Add the onion, chilli, oil, vinegar and ½ teaspoon of fine sea salt, then gently toss to combine. Leave the salad to stand at room temperature for 5–10 minutes, then adjust the salt or vinegar to taste, if necessary (the acid will vary a bit, depending on the juiciness and acidity of the oranges).

Transfer the salad to a shallow serving bowl and sprinkle with the coriander, then crush a few generous pinches of flaky coarse sea salt over the top to taste.

warm beets, walnut-garlic yogurt and fresh mint

Lunching at a Syrian restaurant in Paterson, New Jersey, one chilly winter afternoon, my husband Steve and I dipped warm pieces of torn fresh pitta bread into a flavourful blend of yogurt, garlic and chopped toasted walnuts. That delicious meze inspired this salad, which can be made any time of the year. Use sheeps' milk yogurt if you want an extra tangy flavour, or Greek yogurt for a slightly less lively but creamy taste.

SERVES 4 TO 6

4 medium beetroot (about
   450g), trimmed
50g walnut pieces
1 small garlic clove
½ teaspoon fine sea salt
100ml sheeps' milk yogurt or
   0% fat Greek yogurt
1 tablespoon fresh lemon juice
2½ tablespoons good-quality
   extra virgin olive oil, plus
   more for drizzling
Aleppo chilli flakes or hot chilli
   flakes (see Sources, page 170)
2 tablespoons thinly sliced
   mint leaves
flaky coarse sea salt

Position a rack in the middle of the oven and preheat to 200°C/gas mark 6.

Put the beetroot in a baking dish and add enough water to come about 1cm up the sides of the dish. Cover the dish tightly with foil and roast the beets for 45 minutes – 1 hour or more, depending on size, until tender when pierced with a knife. Uncover and leave to stand until cool enough to peel.

Meanwhile, reduce the oven temperature to 190°C/gas mark 5. Spread the walnut pieces on a baking tray and toast for 5–7 minutes, until lightly golden and fragrant. Transfer to a plate and leave to cool, then coarsely chop.

On a chopping board, cut the garlic clove in half lengthways. If there is a green shoot in the centre, remove and discard it, then coarsely chop the garlic. Form a little mound of the chopped garlic and fine sea salt. Using the blade and the flat side of a chef's knife, alternately chop, mash and scrape the garlic and salt together, until you have a garlic paste. Transfer the paste to a large bowl and add the yogurt, lemon juice and oil, then vigorously whisk the mixture together until the ingredients are well combined. Add about two-thirds of the nuts and a generous pinch of Aleppo chilli flakes. Stir to combine.

Spread the yogurt mixture over the base of a large, shallow serving bowl. Peel and thinly slice the beets crossways, laying the slices over the yogurt. Drizzle generously with oil, then sprinkle with the remaining nuts, mint, a few pinches of chilli flakes and several generous pinches of flaky coarse sea salt.

cooking beets ahead:

It's nice if the beets are still a little warm from the oven when you make this dish, but they can be prepared 1 day ahead and served at room temperature. If you prefer the latter, store the cooled roasted beets unpeeled in an airtight container in the fridge. Bring them to room temperature before peeling, slicing and serving.

pimento cheese with cucumber, spring onion and celery salad

If I had to face the near-impossible task of choosing a favourite Southern food, pimento cheese might have to be it. The sweet creamy spread, especially when home-made, is crazy-delicious comfort fare, as perfect for entertaining as it is between slices of pillow-soft white bread in a lunch-box sandwich. Here it makes a neat and some might say sneaky entrance into the salad world, keeping true to its nature as a comrade to classic crudités. You'll have leftover pimento cheese. If you can resist gobbling it up yourself, it makes a great gift for any food-loving friend or weekend host. The cheese keeps well in a sealed container in the fridge for up to one week. Note: Shop-bought roasted peppers can be used here but roasting your own provides a more vibrant flavour. You can roast the peppers and shred the cheese a day in advance.

PIMENTO CHEESE

2 small–medium red peppers
225g mature Cheddar, grated
3–4 tablespoons mayonnaise
2 tablespoons cream cheese,
   softened at room temperature
freshly ground white pepper
½ teaspoon sugar
¼–½ teaspoon cayenne pepper

SALAD

1 celery heart (4–5 stalks
   with leaves)
120g finely diced peeled
   cucumber (see Box)
1 spring onion, cut crossways
   into 5 pieces, then thinly sliced
   lengthways
freshly ground white pepper
   and fine sea salt
¼ teaspoon white balsamic
   vinegar
¼ teaspoon good-quality extra
   virgin olive oil

12 slightly salty flatbread
   crackers of your choice

To make the pimento cheese, char the peppers over a gas flame, turning frequently, until their skins are blackened and blistered on all sides (or place under a hot grill and cook until the skin is blistered). Transfer to a bowl, cover tightly with cling film and leave to stand for 15 minutes. Rub the skin off the peppers, rinsing your hands under cold running water (but do not rinse the peppers). Remove and discard the cores and every last seed (you can use kitchen paper to gently pat and wipe pepper pieces to help remove the seeds), then finely chop the peppers and place in a large bowl.

Add the Cheddar, mayonnaise, cream cheese, ½ teaspoon of white pepper, the sugar and cayenne pepper. Stir to combine, then cover and chill the pimiento cheese until cold, about 1 hour or up to 1 day.

To make the salad, trim the base of the celery heart. Separate, rinse and dry the stalks, then pinch off and reserve the leaves. Thinly slice the stalks on a slight diagonal. Put the sliced celery in a large bowl. Add 3 packed tablespoons of whole celery leaves, the cucumber and spring onion. Toss together to combine, then add ⅛ teaspoon each of white pepper and salt and toss once more. Add the vinegar and oil and toss to combine.

Remove the pimento cheese from the fridge and spread on top of the crackers. Divide the crackers among 4 serving plates. Mound the salad alongside.

choosing and using cucumbers:

Cucumbers are best when they are juicy, crisp and filled with small, moist, tender seeds. Since the skins of most cucumbers picked for long-distance shipping are treated with wax to retard dehydration, their shiny coating can be a misleading freshness indicator and is also unpalatable. When possible, I purchase cucumbers from farmers' markets – European cucumbers, which have less conspicuous seeds, a thinner skin and a plastic wrapper instead of a wax coating; Kirby cucumbers, which are small with thin, bumpy yellow or green skin and also with inconspicuous seeds; and Persian cucumbers, which are like English cucumbers, only with bumps and don't have to be peeled or seeded. Alternatively, try and buy unwaxed or organic varieties at the supermarket. If you are using a shop-bought cucumber, it's often best to remove and discard the peel. If the seeds are large, they may be dry, bitter or both, in which case scoop them out or cut around and discard them.

sweet pickled peppers and carrots

MAKES 4 SMALL JARS

450g carrots, julienned
2 large red peppers, julienned
240ml cider vinegar
130g sugar
½ teaspoon fine sea salt
¼ teaspoon chilli flakes
¾ teaspoon whole white
   peppercorns, crushed
15g coarsely chopped fresh
   coriander

I use this pickle as both a condiment and a mini salad to eat on its own, or pair it with other salads or cooked meats and fish. It's great with barbecued foods, as a cocktail snack or as part of a meal of small plates. It's also terrific with oozy cheeses, in fish or pork tacos and alongside a tuna salad.

In a large frying pan, combine the carrots, peppers, 320ml cold water, vinegar, sugar, salt, chilli flakes and peppercorns. Bring to the boil over a high heat, then reduce to a gentle simmer and cook, stirring occasionally, for about 20 minutes, until the vegetables are tender but still have texture.

Remove the frying pan from the heat and leave to stand for 10 minutes, then transfer the contents to a serving bowl. Stir in the coriander.

Note: This keeps well for several days in the fridge and the flavours deepen over time. If you make it ahead, bring it to room temperature before serving.

tomatoes, smoked mozzarella and lemon

SERVES 4

1 lemon
1 tablespoon finely chopped
   shallots
¼ teaspoon fine sea salt
680g tomatoes (a mix of large
   and small varieties if you like)
225g scamorza cheese
   (scamorza affumicata) or
   smoked mozzarella, cubed
1 celery stalk, thinly sliced
3 tablespoons good-quality
   extra virgin olive oil, plus
   more for drizzling
flaky coarse sea salt
¾ teaspoon whole black
   peppercorns, crushed

This is not your typical tomato and mozzarella salad: it includes a smoked mozzarella rather than the plain type, and it's paired with quickly cured strips of lemon rind in place of basil. Save this and any other tomato salad for late summer and early autumn, when tomatoes are replete with sweet juices. Use the best in-season tomatoes you can find.

Using a sharp vegetable peeler (or a sharp paring knife), remove the peel from the lemon, avoiding the white pith. Then, using a chef's knife, very thinly slice the rind.

Squeeze the lemon to make 1 tablespoon of juice. In a small bowl, stir together the rind and juice, shallots and fine sea salt. Leave to stand for 10 minutes.

Meanwhile, cut the tomatoes in halves or quarters, depending on their size. Combine with the cheese and celery in a large serving bowl.

Add the oil to the shallot and lemon mixture, stirring to combine. Spoon the mixture over the tomatoes, then crush several generous pinches of flaky coarse sea salt over the top and sprinkle with the crushed pepper. Toss everything together, then drizzle the salad with a little extra oil if desired.

shredded celeriac, manchego cheese and pistachios

Although milder than celery, celeriac has a robust flavour and extremely crunchy texture when first peeled and cut. Once it has marinated with good olive oil and salt for a short time, the root softens and its flavour mingles with the other ingredients of the salad while still retaining its character and crunch.

SERVES 4

570g celeriac, trimmed
  and peeled
25g flat-leaf parsley leaves
120ml good-quality extra
  virgin olive oil, plus more
  for drizzling
flaky coarse sea salt
150g Manchego cheese,
  thinly shaved
35g shelled unsalted pistachios,
  coarsely chopped
freshly ground black pepper

If you have one large whole celeriac, cut it in half or quarters to make slicing easier. Using a mandoline, cut the celeriac into 3mm-thick strips (julienne) then put them into a large bowl.

Add the parsley and oil, then crush ¾ teaspoon of salt over the top and toss well to combine. Cover the bowl with cling film and leave to stand at room temperature for 1 hour, or place in the fridge for up to 4 hours. (If chilling, about 45 minutes before serving time, transfer the mixture to a clean bowl, using a rubber spatula to scrape the oil and salt from the cold bowl, and allow to come to room temperature before proceeding.)

Add the cheese and nuts to the celeriac mixture and toss to combine. Season generously with salt and pepper then spoon onto serving plates and drizzle with oil.

shaved brussels sprouts, olive oil, lemon and peppered sheeps' milk cheese

Very thinly sliced raw Brussels sprouts tossed with lots of good-quality extra virgin olive oil, zingy fresh lemon juice and a peppery and slightly tart aged sheeps' cheese is enough to convert even the most ardent sprouts–averse folk. Try it when Brussels sprouts are in season, from late August to March, and see for yourself. This salad is best served immediately as it loses its lemony punch if it sits for too long.

SERVES 4 TO 6

450g Brussels sprouts
5 tablespoons good-quality
  extra virgin olive oil
½ teaspoon fine sea salt
3½ tablespoons fresh
  lemon juice
½ teaspoon whole black
  peppercorns, crushed
115g semi-soft pecorino
  cheese studded with black
  peppercorns, very thinly
  shaved (see Box)

Rinse the Brussels sprouts, then pat dry with kitchen paper. Remove any outer leaves that have brown spots or have yellowed, then cut the sprouts in half, lengthwise. Very thinly slice the sprouts crosswise, transferring the sliced pieces to a large shallow serving bowl as you go. Discard the stems.

Drizzle the oil over the sprouts, then sprinkle with the salt and toss well to combine. Add the lemon juice, then the crushed pepper and toss once more. Lay the cheese over the top of the salad and serve immediately.

about semi-soft pecorino cheese:

In speciality cheese shops and delicatessens, you may find semi-soft pecorino cheese studded with piquant black peppercorns; it will often be labelled *rustico*. If you can't find one with peppercorns, add more crushed peppercorns to this dish.

roasted spiced cauliflower with rocket

Rocket leaves are used almost like a herb here, an extra rather than the main attraction; they bring a green and slightly peppery note to the dish. If you like coriander, try swapping a generous handful or two of whole leaves for the rocket. A nice warm or room-temperature dish, this also makes a great side for grilled fish or lamb chops. I prefer baby or wild rocket for this salad, but if you can't find it, remove the stems and tear the leaves of larger rocket.

SERVES 4

1 large head cauliflower
    (about 1kg), broken up into
    small florets
60ml plus 2 tablespoons
    extra virgin olive oil
flaky coarse sea salt
¼ teaspoon ground cumin
Aleppo chilli flakes, piment
    d'Espelette powder or a thinly
    sliced medium-hot fresh chilli,
    e.g. serrano (see Sources,
    page 170)
3 medium red onions, peeled
    and cut lengthways into wedges
1 navel orange
3 tablespoons pine nuts
85g baby or wild rocket

Position a rack in the middle of the oven and preheat to 200°C/gas mark 6. Line a rimmed baking tray with baking paper.

In a large bowl, toss together the cauliflower, 60ml oil, ¼ teaspoon of salt, ⅛ teaspoon of cumin and a few generous pinches of Aleppo chilli flakes. Reserving the mixing bowl, spread the cauliflower onto the prepared baking sheet and roast for 15 minutes.

Meanwhile, put the onions into the mixing bowl. Add the remaining 2 tablespoons of oil, ¼ teaspoon of salt, ⅛ teaspoon of cumin, and a few generous pinches of Aleppo chilli flakes.

Remove the tray from the oven. Add the onion mixture to the tray, scraping the bowl with a rubber spatula to drizzle any oil and spices over the vegetables, then arrange the vegetables in a single layer. If any cauliflower pieces are browned on the bottom, turn them and move them to the centre of the tray (vegetables on the edges of the tray will brown faster than those in the centre).

Return the tray to the oven and roast for a further 20 minutes, then stir the vegetables and continue to roast for about 5 minutes until tender and golden. Transfer the tray to a wire rack, then finely zest about one-third of the orange rind over the vegetables, holding the zester a few centimetres above the tray so that you capture the flavourful oil that sprays from the orange as you zest.

In a heavy frying pan over a medium heat, toast the pine nuts for about 4–6 minutes, stirring occasionally, until fragrant and lightly golden, Transfer the nuts to a large serving bowl. Add the cauliflower and onions, scraping any oil and spices from the tray into the serving bowl, then add the rocket and toss to combine. Season with salt and Aleppo chilli flakes to taste. Serve warm or at room temperature.

fresh figs, shaved celery and prosciutto

The combination of sweet fresh figs and salty prosciutto is a serious treat. A small mound of celery salad alongside the classic duo turns this into a great plate to pair with wine or cocktails, a sweet little meal on its own, or a nice start to a larger feast.

SERVES 4

1 celery heart (5–6 stalks
  with leaves)
3 tablespoons snipped chives
3 tablespoons good-quality
  extra virgin olive oil, plus
  more for drizzling
flaky coarse sea salt
1 lemon
8 thin slices prosciutto di Parma
8 fresh figs, stems trimmed,
  halved (see Box)

Trim the base of the celery heart. Separate, rinse and dry the stalks, then pinch off and reserve the leaves. Thinly slice the stalks on a slight diagonal.

Transfer the celery slices and leaves to a large bowl. Add the chives, oil and crush a few generous pinches of salt over the top, then finely grate the zest from the lemon into the bowl, holding the zester close to the bowl so that you capture the flavourful oil that sprays from the lemon as you zest. Toss to combine, then leave to stand for 5 minutes to allow the celery to wilt slightly. Toss the salad again and adjust the seasoning if desired.

Lay the prosciutto on serving plates, leaving room for the figs and salad. Divide the figs, cut sides up, among the plates. Lightly season the figs with salt. Mound the celery salad onto the plates. Drizzle the figs and salad with a touch of oil.

choosing and using fresh figs:

Ripe, fresh figs are plump and yield slightly to pressure; they store well loosely covered in the fridge for up to three days. Slightly underripe figs can be ripened on a plate at room temperature for a day or two. Overripe or bruised fruit will be mushy and have a soured scent. Fresh fig season runs from summer and through much of autumn. To wash figs, simply rinse and gently pat dry.

artichokes with radicchio and white anchovies

If you loathe anchovies but haven't tried white anchovies, you owe it to yourself to give them a go. Known as *boquerones* in Spain and *alici* in Italy, fresh white anchovies are milder in flavour than their tinned cured counterparts and not at all fishy or salty. Packed with beneficial omega-3 fatty acids, the delicate little fish taste slightly tangy as they are sold in oil, often with a touch of white vinegar and herbs. If you want to make this dish without anchovies, you may find it needs an extra squeeze of lemon.

SERVES 4 TO 6

2–3 lemons
680g baby artichokes
60ml good-quality extra
  virgin olive oil
flaky coarse sea salt
1 small head radicchio, leaves
  separated and torn into bite-
  sized pieces
85g Parmigiano-Reggiano
  cheese, thinly shaved
12 white anchovy fillets
  (see Sources, page 170)
1 teaspoon whole black
  peppercorns, crushed

Fill a large bowl halfway up with very cold water and a few ice cubes. Squeeze the juice of 1 lemon through a fine-mesh sieve into the bowl, discarding the seeds.

Trim away the tough outer leaves of 1 artichoke to expose its tender pale green interior. Using a serrated knife, cut off the top third of the artichoke, then use a vegetable peeler to remove the tough outer layers around the base and stem. Trim 3mm or so of the stem. Cut the artichoke in half lengthways (if you see any signs of a hairy choke in the centre, dig it out with a small spoon). Using a sharp chef's knife, cut the artichoke lengthways into 3mm slices then transfer the slices into the prepared water. Repeat with the remaining artichokes.

Squeeze the remaining lemons to make 3 tablespoons of juice. Drain the sliced artichokes and pat dry, then transfer to a large bowl. Add the oil, then crush 1 teaspoon of flaky coarse sea salt over the artichoke slices and toss well to combine. Add the radicchio and lemon juice, and toss once more. Adjust the salt, if necessary. Divide the salad among serving plates, then top with the cheese shavings, anchovies and black pepper.

blueberries, feta and mint

This beautiful and unexpected combination is one of my favourite ways to surprise lunch or dinner guests, as blueberries don't often show up in salads or the savoury parts of a meal. It's terrific as a little salad to start a meal and works well as a cheese or savoury dessert course too. It is also tasty spooned over lamb chops – the gamier the better. Serve this salad from late spring to early autumn, when blueberries are in season and at their best. Grab a box from your local farmers' market or you can also grow the fruit yourself – those grown in colder climates have a better flavour.

SERVES 4

400g blueberries
20g mint leaves, large
  leaves torn
150g feta cheese, crumbled
4 tablespoons good-quality
  extra virgin olive oil
flaky coarse sea salt
1 teaspoon whole black
  peppercorns, crushed

Divide the blueberries among small, shallow serving bowls, then sprinkle with the mint and cheese. Drizzle 1 tablespoon of the oil over each serving. Crush several generous pinches of salt over each dish and sprinkle with black pepper.

sprouts and avocado salad with cold-pressed pumpkin seed oil

Adzuki, radish, lentil, chickpea, clover, sunflower, mustard, pea and snow pea are just a few of the sprout varieties that make this salad shine. Pre-packed boxes of mixed sprouts can be found in most good health food shops. Paired with a creamy ripe avocado, the variety of sprout flavours is unique and exciting.

SERVES 4

340g mixed sprouts
1 large firm, ripe avocado
flaky coarse sea salt
60ml cold-pressed pumpkin or
    other squash seed oil (see Box)
3 tablespoons fresh lemon juice

Divide the sprouts among 4 serving plates. Cut the avocado into quarters lengthways, then remove the pit and peel. Cut the pieces lengthways into 5mm-thick slices, then arrange the slices alongside the sprouts.

Crush several generous pinches of salt over the sprouts and avocado slices, then drizzle each salad with the oil and lemon juice.

in praise of squash seed oils:

Pumpkin seed oil lends a delicious nutty flavour to salads, and is packed with nutrients, including omega-3 and omega-6 fatty acids (aka good fats), plus vitamins A, C and E. I recommend a cold-pressed oil here since, as with all oils produced for consumption, cold-pressed varieties are significantly higher in quality and more flavourful and nutritious than oils that are extracted using heat. Other squash seed oils (acorn, delicata, butternut, etc.) are also wonderful and have similar nutritional benefits. (See Sources, page 170.)

asparagus mimosa with capers, radishes and chives

Adding a few flourishes to the classic pairing of asparagus and grated egg turns it into more of a salad. A nice light meal on its own, this dish can also kick off or be part of a larger affair.

SERVES 4

2 medium eggs
2 medium–large radishes,
   very thinly sliced
3 tablespoons, plus 1 teaspoon
   good-quality extra virgin
   olive oil
fine sea salt and freshly ground
   black pepper
680g asparagus, trimmed
2 tablespoons finely chopped
   chives
1 tablespoon capers, preferably
   salt-packed (see Box)
Aleppo chilli flakes, piment
   d'Espelette chilli powder
   or a thinly sliced fresh
   medium-hot chilli, e.g. serrano
   (see Sources, page 170)
1 lemon, cut into wedges

Place the eggs in a small saucepan with enough cold water to cover them by 5cm and heat until just boiling. Remove the pan from the heat and leave to stand, covered, for 8 minutes.

Rinse the capers and then soak them in cold water for 10 minutes. Rinse again and coarsely chop.

Meanwhile, place the radish slices in a small bowl, add 1 teaspoon of oil and a generous pinch or two of fine sea salt and pepper, and toss to combine.

Drain the eggs and submerge them in a small bowl of very cold water and a few ice cubes for a few minutes, then peel. Coarsely chop the eggs.

Fill a large frying pan with enough water to come three-quarters the way up the sides of the pan. Add salt and bring to the boil. Add the asparagus and cook until just tender, about 3½ minutes for medium spears. Drain, transfer to a large bowl and, while hot, toss with the remaining 3 tablespoons of oil and a generous pinch of fine sea salt.

Transfer the asparagus to serving plates. Drizzle any oil left in the mixing bowl on top. Top with the radishes, egg, chives, capers and a generous pinch or two of chilli. Serve immediately with lemon wedges for squeezing.

try out salt-packed capers:

Those who know me well know my penchant for salt-packed capers over ones that are jarred in vinegar. The salted sort is plumper, meatier in texture and livelier in flavour than the vinegar-brined kind. Certainly worth a taste test of your own, especially if you haven't tried them before. (See Sources, page 170.)

summer tomatoes, fresh herb leaves and barely pickled red onion

When summer tomatoes finally arrive, I keep a bowl of mixed varieties at the ready; they seem to make their way into nearly every meal of the day. Any type of good fresh tomato works well in this salad, but if possible use a mix of heritage tomatoes, such as Black Russian, Gardeners Delight or San Marzano. Also try an unusual cucumber, such as the sweet round yellow variety that can be eaten like an apple or the mildly flavoured Lebanese with crisp, pale green flesh. These might be found in farmers' markets, some larger supermarkets and specialist green grocers. For more on cucumbers, see page 23.

SERVES 4 TO 6

1 small red onion, halved and
  very thinly sliced
1 tablespoon red wine vinegar
fine sea salt
1kg mixed heritage tomatoes,
  cut into 5mm wedges
1 medium cucumber, or
  2–3 Persian cucumbers,
  very thinly sliced crossways
20g combination of mint, basil
  and/or tarragon leaves
2 tablespoons snipped chives
flaky coarse sea salt
good-quality extra virgin olive
  oil for drizzling

In a small bowl, toss together the onion, vinegar and ¼ teaspoon of salt. Leave to stand for 10 minutes then drain, discarding the vinegar.

In a large serving bowl, arrange the tomatoes and cucumber. Scatter the marinated onion, herb leaves and chives over the salad. Crush several generous pinches of flaky coarse sea salt over the top then drizzle liberally with oil.

to barely pickle:

The thin slices of red onions in this salad are pickled ever so slightly in a little vinegar and salt. There's just enough acid to tone down the bite of the onion, which some people find too harsh, without adding a strong vinegar flavour or dressing. This allows the tomatoes to provide their own acidity and juicy, bright flavours.

honeydew melon, sweet green peppers and ricotta salata

This salad of melon, sweet pepper, salty cheese and earthy basil recalls the watermelon salad that we all love so much, but its elegant components make it more refined. Salt is key to marrying the flavours so be generous, tasting as you go. Be liberal with the extra virgin olive oil too – it's very much a part of this salad.

SERVES 4

½ honeydew melon
2 small–medium sweet Italian or
   banana peppers (see Box)
flaky coarse sea salt
20g basil leaves, large ones torn
115g ricotta salata cheese,
   thinly sliced
good-quality extra virgin
   olive oil for drizzling

Scoop the seeds out of the melon and remove the peel. Cut it in half lengthways, then thinly slice crossways on a diagonal. Trim and deseed the chillies, then thinly slice them crossways into rings.

On a large platter, arrange a layer of slightly overlapping melon slices and season with generous pinches of salt. Add layers of the chilli rings, basil leaves and ricotta slices. If layering a second round, remember to season with salt between the layers of melon. Sprinkle several generous pinches of salt over the top of the salad, then drizzle liberally with oil. Serve immediately.

picking the perfect chilli pepper:

Italian sweet peppers are long and tapered and taste mild and sweet. Banana peppers make a good substitute, but be sure to taste first – I prefer a sweet rather than hot pepper for this dish. (Note: Banana peppers resemble their semi-fiery cousin, the Hungarian wax pepper, so it's easy to bring home the heat when you are really looking for the sweet.)

watermelon salad with feta cheese, fresh herb leaves and two chillies

Myriad versions of this salad abound, yet it's so good – especially with the heat of both fresh and dried chillies – that I didn't want to miss the chance to include it in this book. Roasted pumpkin seeds (also known as pepitas) lend a little crunch. I like to use a hot chilli here, such as Scotch bonnet, but if your tastes run milder, try a deseeded serrano instead. Coarsely crushed black peppercorns or crushed chilli flakes make a fine stand-in for the more exotic and interesting Aleppo chilli or piment d'Espelette, if necessary. Use a fruity-style oil here to complement the melon, or a grassy, piquant variety for a little extra kick.

SERVES 4 TO 6

1.8kg seedless watermelon, peel removed, cut into 0.5cm cubes
140g feta cheese, crumbled
10g coriander leaves
5g mint leaves, torn into small pieces
1 fresh hot chilli, e.g. Scotch bonnet, deseeded and very thinly sliced
Aleppo chilli flakes or piment d'Espelette powder (see Sources, page 170)
flaky coarse sea salt
50g roasted shelled pumpkin seeds (pepitas)
60ml good-quality extra virgin olive oil, plus more for drizzling
juice of 1 lime

In a large, shallow serving bowl, layer half of the watermelon then scatter over half of the feta, coriander, mint and fresh chilli. Season with a generous sprinkle of Aleppo chilli flakes and several generous pinches of salt. Sprinkle with half of the pumpkin seeds then drizzle with half of the oil and half of the lime juice.

Repeat with the remaining ingredients. Drizzle with a little extra oil, if desired.

courgette and radish with lime

When thinly sliced, raw courgette is sweet and tender, yet still holds a nice bit of crunch. The liberal use of lime juice really peps things up here, bringing a spark to this extremely versatile little salad. I love it served in small dishes with a good cocktail to kick off a spring or summer dinner party, but it's also terrific as a salad on its own, or piled into pitta bread with warm shredded roast chicken or on top of a burger (or a piece of grilled fish or pork chop or...) any time of the year.

SERVES 4

1 tablespoon finely chopped
  shallot
1½ tablespoons fresh lime juice
fine sea salt
450g small–medium courgettes
4 medium–large radishes
2 tablespoons good-quality
  extra virgin olive oil
2 tablespoons coarsely chopped
  coriander
flaky coarse sea salt

In a small bowl, stir together the shallot, lime juice and ¼ teaspoon of fine sea salt. Leave to stand for 10–15 minutes.

Meanwhile, trim the ends of the courgettes on a slight diagonal, then cut crossways into very thin slices, preferably using a mandoline on its thinnest setting (see Box). Transfer the courgette slices to a bowl then prepare the radishes in the same way. Add the oil and ½ teaspoon of fine sea salt to the vegetables and toss to combine. Add the lime juice mixture and toss once more.

Transfer the salad to a serving bowl, ensuring you drizzle with any leftover juices. Sprinkle with the coriander and a couple of generous pinches of flaky coarse sea salt.

the art of slicing:

It is best to use a mandoline to slice the courgettes and radishes for this recipe. While a fancy mandoline is a nice tool to have, the plastic types are inexpensive – a good one costs around £30 – and widely available (see Sources, page 170). Slicers come with a guard and it's best to always use it, to avoid both food waste and injuries. If the radishes are small, use a few more than called for here, and be extra careful when slicing.

raw mushroom salad with garlic and fresh herbs

This quick and simple mushroom salad is commonplace in Italy, where you might find it made with fresh porcini when they're in season. Here I suggest a mix of button, enoki, chanterelle and porcini mushrooms, but use whatever you can find or forage. The mushrooms absorb quite a bit of the oil, so this salad will be a bit drier than most. Slicing them thinly helps them to absorb less and also makes for a more subtle texture and elegant flavour. A little carafe of oil can be served on the side if you like.

SERVES 4

120ml good-quality extra
  virgin olive oil
1 garlic clove, peeled and cut
  into 4 long, thin slices
fine sea salt
450g mixed mushrooms
  (see Box)
3 tablespoons very thinly sliced
  mint leaves
1 tablespoon finely chopped
  chives
1 tablespoon finely chopped basil
freshly ground black pepper

In a small bowl, whisk together the oil, garlic and ¼ teaspoon of sea salt. Leave the mixture to stand while you prepare the mushrooms.

If you are using shiitakes, remove and discard the stalks or save them for making a broth. Trim the base of button, chanterelle and porcini mushroom stalks, and very thinly slice both tops and stalks lengthways. If you are using enoki mushrooms, separate the clusters at their base into individual mushrooms or clusters of two or three.

On large serving plates, spread the sliced mushrooms in a single layer, overlapping a little. Scatter over the enoki mushrooms (if using), followed by the mint, chives and basil, then season generously with salt and pepper. Just before serving, whisk the oil mixture again, then drizzle it over the salad. Serve immediately.

much ado about mushrooms:

Mushrooms seem to be one of the foods that divide people into two camps: like them or hate them. I like mushrooms very much; I generally prefer them raw over cooked and in salads, they seem to be at their most delicate when very thinly sliced. The stems of most mushrooms you would eat raw can also be very thinly sliced and enjoyed uncooked, just trim the bottom before slicing. Shiitake stems are a bit tough so I don't tend to eat them raw but they are great thinly sliced and added to soups, or used whole to make broths. When purchasing, choose mushrooms that are firm, unbruised and have closed 'veils – the area where the cap and stem meet. For enokis, look for firm, white, shiny caps and firm stalks.

pimento peppers with tuna, capers and fresh herbs

SERVES 4

1½ tablespoons capers,
   preferably salt-packed (see
   Box, page 32)
280g good-quality tuna in oil
3 tablespoons mayonnaise
1 spring onion, white and green
   parts only, thinly sliced,
   plus more for garnish
2 tablespoons thinly sliced basil
   leaves, plus more for garnish
1 teaspoon Dijon mustard
½ teaspoon white wine vinegar
¼ teaspoon fine sea salt
piment d'Espelette or freshly
   ground black pepper
1 x 185g tin whole roasted
   pimento peppers (see Box)
good-quality extra virgin olive
   oil for drizzling

This dish reminds my husband Steve of his childhood days in Seville, Spain, where he spent mornings shopping in the open-air markets with his mum and brother while his dad, a Spanish history professor, conducted research. The pimiento peppers surely recall food memories, but I think it's also the nature of this extremely simple and richly flavoured recipe, which is equally satisfying for a lunch or a tapas before dinner.

Rinse the capers, soak them in cold water for 10 minutes, then rinse again and coarsely chop them.

Drain and place the tuna in a large bowl. Flake with a fork to break up the larger pieces. Add the mayonnaise, spring onion, basil, capers, mustard, vinegar, the salt and a generous pinch of piment d'Espelette or freshly ground black pepper. Stir to combine.

Drain the peppers, then hold one, with the opening facing up like an ice cream cone, in your non-dominant hand. With the other hand, drop pinches of the tuna mixture into the cavity of the pepper until it is full to the top. Transfer the filled pepper to a serving plate and repeat with the remaining peppers. If you have any leftover tuna, serve it mounded in the centre of the plate or in a separate bowl (or save it for later). Drizzle the filled peppers and the plate with oil and sprinkle with spring onion, basil and piment d'Espelette.

about roasted pimento peppers:

Pimento is the Spanish word for 'pepper' and the name you will find on canned and jarred roasted peppers from Spain. Though you can use roasted red bell peppers here, the pimientos are best, because of their smaller size and sweeter, richer flavor. You can buy roasted pimientos in jars (packed in water) or in tins (packed in oil). Avoid those with vinegar added; it is easier to control the flavour of your dish when you start with a pure pepper and then have the option to add your own good-quality vinegar. If you are purchasing a European brand, a 185-gram tin gives you the equivalent product to the 6½-ounce jar that is specified in this recipe.

tender carrots with miso and tahini

Big thanks go to my friend, Linsey Herman, for helping me to perfect this recipe. I appreciate her keen taste for flavour balance, especially with Asian ingredients, and her brilliant addition of honey. You'll find miso paste in health food shops, delis and some supermarkets as well as online.

SERVES 4

450g medium–large carrots
2 teaspoons tahini
2 tablespoons white or yellow
  miso paste
1 tablespoon, plus 1 teaspoon
  fresh lemon juice
1 tablespoon good-quality
  extra virgin olive oil
1 teaspoon honey
¼ teaspoon finely chopped garlic
¼ teaspoon finely chopped
  fresh ginger
¼ teaspoon soy sauce
fine sea salt and freshly ground
  black pepper
10g coarsely chopped coriander
2 tablespoons thinly sliced
  mint leaves

Bring a large saucepan of salted water to the boil. Meanwhile, using an adjustable-blade slicer, shred the carrots into 3mm-thick matchsticks (or carefully cut by hand using a good sharp chef's knife, carefully). Blanch the carrots for about 1½ minutes, until just tender, then run under cold water, drain and pat dry with kitchen paper.

In a large mixing bowl, whisk together the tahini, miso paste, 2 tablespoons of warm water, lemon juice, olive oil, honey, garlic, ginger, soy sauce and a pinch each of salt and pepper. Add the carrots and toss to combine and evenly coat, then add the coriander and mint, and toss once more. Adjust the seasoning if desired.

roasted aubergine and tomatoes with cashew-parsley pesto

It's fun to mix things up during a meal by serving roasted vegetables as a salad. Using pesto as a dressing can also be new and delicious, whether as I do here or by serving a looser pesto over greens, as you'll see in the next chapter. The cheese is optional here for those with dietary restrictions and because the pesto is delicious either way.

SERVES 4

PESTO
30g parsley leaves
25g basil leaves
30g roasted unsalted cashews
1 tablespoon snipped chives
1 medium garlic clove,
  cut in half
60ml plus 2 tablespoons
  good-quality extra virgin
  olive oil

1 lemon
2 tablespoons finely grated
  Parmigiano-Reggiano
  (optional)

fine sea salt and freshly ground
  black pepper
580–680g aubergine or
  Italian aubergine, cut into
  2.5cm cubes

580–680g cocktail or cherry
  tomatoes, or a mix
60ml plus 2 tablespoons extra
  virgin olive oil
fine sea salt and freshly ground
  black pepper
good-quality extra virgin olive oil
  for drizzling
flaky coarse sea salt

Position racks in the middle and upper third of the oven and preheat to 220°C/gas mark 7. Line 2 rimmed baking trays with baking paper.

To make the pesto, place the parsley, basil, cashews, chives and garlic in a food processor and purée, stopping to scrape the sides of the bowl if necessary. With the machine running, add 60ml oil in a slow, steady stream, until the pesto is smooth and the ingredients are incorporated.

Transfer the pesto to a bowl. Finely grate the zest from the lemon into the bowl, holding the zester close so that you capture the flavourful oil, then juice enough of the lemon to make 1 teaspoon. Stir in the lemon juice, the remaining 2 tablespoons of oil and the cheese, if using. Season with ½–¾ teaspoon of salt and pepper to taste.

Spread the aubergine and tomatoes in a single layer on each of the baking trays and drizzle with the oil. Season with the fine sea salt and black pepper. Roast, rotating the trays halfway through, until the tomatoes have burst but still hold their shape and the aubergine is tender.

Divide the pesto among 4 serving plates and spread to an even, thin layer. Spoon the aubergine and tomatoes on top, drizzle with the finishing oil and sprinkle with a pinch or two of flaky coarse sea salt.

chapter two:

LEAF SALADS

red cabbage, green apple and sweet currant coleslaw

This crisp, bright winter coleslaw, with its hint of sweet-tart fruit and nutty seeds, provides a lively contrast to the hearty roasts, soups and braised dishes that keep us fortified throughout the chilly season.

SERVES 4

1 large Granny Smith apple
400g very thinly sliced
    red cabbage
35g roasted and unsalted
    sunflower seeds
30g currants
3 tablespoons good-quality extra
    virgin olive oil
1½ tablespoons cider vinegar
flaky coarse sea salt and freshly
    ground black pepper

Cut the apple from its core, then discard the core. Thinly slice the apple pieces lengthways and place them in a large serving bowl. Add the cabbage, sunflower seeds and currants, and toss to combine.

Drizzle over the olive oil and vinegar, and sprinkle with 1½ teaspoons of salt. Add ½ teaspoon of black pepper, then toss to combine. Adjust the seasoning, if necessary.

never the same slaw twice:

Once November comes round, Steve and I begin to accept and even welcome winter's short days and brisk weather. It's always a surprise how many variations we come up with for our winter coleslaws, most of which tend to be spontaneously cobbled together with a mix of fridge and store cupboard items. Here are some tips for spur-of-the-moment coleslaws. Any combination of nuts, seeds, cheese, fresh or dried fruit and crunchy winter vegetables works well. Not all categories need to be included, and ingredients can be numerous or not. Vinegars can be varied as you wish. We generally begin with a base of red or green cabbage and add from there. Think cashews, toasted walnuts, pumpkin seeds, pistachios or crushed peanuts in place of sunflower seeds; orange segments, diced mango, julienned papaya, sliced kumquats, a crisp pear such as Concorde, or any apple variety in place of the Granny Smith; shredded carrot, sliced kohlrabi, celery or fennel and baby rocket to add colour and more texture; fresh herbs or celery leaves to add brightness or maybe even match the dish to a Mexican, Mediterranean or Indian meal; or shards of aged Cheddar, Grana Padano or a tangy semi-soft goats' cheese for a more complex and filling dish with a bit of protein.

red oak lettuce with spiced popcorn, drunken cherries and goats' gouda

My version of cereal for dinner – when I'm too tired to cook and a takeaway is not an option – is a simple salad or a big bowl of popcorn. As it turns out, the two work well together. Like nuts and seeds, popcorn can be sprinkled over salads to add flavour and an exciting textural element. Here, a peppery-spiced version is the perfect complement to boozy cherries. Red oak lettuce's tender leaves, shaped like those of an oak tree, lend a pleasing hint of bitter. If the greens are not available, try a mix of sliced chicory and any sort of tender lettuce.

240ml dry red wine
70g dried sour cherries
4 leafy thyme sprigs
1 teaspoon sugar
freshly ground black pepper and
   fine sea salt
⅛ teaspoon cayenne pepper
50g popcorn kernels
2 tablespoons vegetable oil
½ teaspoon red wine vinegar
¼ teaspoon Dijon mustard
3 tablespoons good-quality
   extra virgin olive oil
225g red oak lettuce
55g goats' milk Gouda,
   freshly grated

In a small saucepan, combine the wine, cherries, thyme, sugar, ¼ teaspoon of black pepper and ⅛ teaspoon of salt. Gently simmer the mixture over a medium-low heat for 20–25 minutes, stirring occasionally and reducing the heat if necessary, until the cherries are plump and the wine is reduced to 2 tablespoons.

Meanwhile, in a small bowl, stir together ¼ teaspoon of salt, ¼ teaspoon of black pepper and the cayenne pepper, then set aside. Combine the popcorn kernels and vegetable oil in a large, deep pan with a lid. Place over a medium-high heat for about 2 minutes until the oil is hot, occasionally swirling the pan to coat the kernels with oil, and then cover the pan. When the popcorn kernels start popping, occasionally shake the pan back and forth over the heat until all the kernels have popped. Transfer to a large bowl. Immediately sprinkle the reserved spice mixture over the top and, using 2 large spoons, toss the popcorn to distribute the spices.

When the cherries are ready, strain the liquid through a fine-mesh sieve into a large serving bowl. Spread the cherries on a plate, discarding the thyme.

Add the vinegar, mustard, ⅛ teaspoon of salt and ⅛ teaspoon of black pepper to the serving bowl and whisk to combine, then add the oil and vigorously whisk until the dressing is emulsified.

Separate the lettuce leaves, tearing the larger pieces into bite-sized pieces. Add the lettuce to the bowl with the dressing and toss to coat, then add the popcorn and toss once more. Taste and adjust the seasoning, if necessary. Distribute the salad among serving plates, then top with the cherries and grated cheese.

chicory salad with toasted walnuts and concorde pear

Pecorino Toscano cheese provides a sweet, milky contrast to the slight bitterness of the chicory in this salad. Avoid tossing pecorino Romano in your trolley in place of the much milder, less salty and more refined pecorino Toscano. The cheeses are not interchangeable. If the Toscano is not available, choose a good Parmigiano-Reggiano or Grana Padano instead.

SERVES 4

100g walnut pieces
1 Concorde pear
450g chicory
55g pecorino Toscano
3 tablespoons good-quality
   extra virgin olive oil
2 tablespoons finely chopped
   chives
1 tablespoon white balsamic
   vinegar
fine sea salt and freshly ground
   black pepper

Preheat the oven to 180°C/gas mark 4. Spread the nuts on a baking tray and bake for 8–12 minutes, stirring once or twice, until fragrant and lightly toasted.

Meanwhile, core and thinly slice the pear and put the slices in a large serving bowl. Cut the chicory crossways on a diagonal into 5mm-thick slices, then add to the serving bowl.

When the nuts are toasted, remove them from the oven and transfer to a plate. Allow the nuts to cool for about 5 minutes, then coarsely chop and add to the serving bowl.

Using a vegetable peeler, slice the cheese into very thin shards. Add to the serving bowl with the oil, chives, vinegar, ¾ teaspoon of salt and ½ teaspoon of black pepper. Toss together to combine.

shaved fennel and rocket salad with lemon-olive pesto and toasted pine nuts

The assertive, tangy dressing for this salad comes from the pages of *La Cucina Italiana* magazine, where I am the food editor. In the magazine, it originally played a starring role as a pesto for drizzling over bass crudo, which is thinly sliced, very fresh raw bass. It is terrific on fish, raw or gently cooked, and as a pesto for wholewheat or ordinary pasta, served warm or cold. But it also makes a delicious vinaigrette, as I found out when, in need of a salad for my friend Carol's birthday dinner, I served it this way and it was met with applause.

SERVES 4

3 tablespoons pine nuts
1 lemon
25g basil leaves
4 tablespoons good-quality extra
  virgin olive oil
50g stoned Gaeta olives
fine sea salt and freshly ground
  black pepper
225g baby rocket
1 large fennel bulb, very thinly
  sliced crossways

Toast the pine nuts in a dry heavy-based frying pan over a medium-low heat for 4–6 minutes, stirring occasionally, until fragrant and a shade or two darker. Transfer the nuts to a plate to cool.

Using a sharp vegetable peeler, remove 2 long, wide strips of zest from the lemon, avoiding the white pith. Squeeze the lemon to make 1½ tablespoons of juice.

In a blender, combine the lemon zest and juice, basil, oil, 25g of the olives, ⅛ teaspoon of salt and a generous pinch of pepper. Purée the dressing until smooth.

Quarter the remaining 25g of the olives lengthways. In a large serving bowl, gently toss together half of the nuts, the rocket, fennel, ½ teaspoon of salt and ¼ teaspoon of black pepper. Drizzle with the dressing and sprinkle with the olives and remaining nuts.

cress, avocado and grapefruit salad with tarragon-shallot vinaigrette

Grapefruits, especially pink ones when available, do a wonderful job of bringing a sense of warmth to a chilly winter day. Here, their sweet-tart juices also brighten the peppery flavour of the watercress. If you don't have Champagne vinegar on hand, a good white wine one will do.

SERVES 4

VINAIGRETTE

1 tablespoon finely chopped shallot

1 tablespoon Champagne vinegar

fine sea salt

1 teaspoon white peppercorns, crushed (see Box)

3 tablespoons good-quality extra virgin olive oil

2 teaspoons finely chopped tarragon plus 2 tablespoons whole leaves for garnish

1 large or 2 small pink or ruby grapefruits

1 firm, ripe avocado (see Box, page 165)

large bunch of watercress, thin stems and leaves only

flaky coarse sea salt

To make the base for the dressing, in a medium bowl, stir together the shallot, vinegar, ¼ teaspoon of fine sea salt and ¾ teaspoon of white pepper and leave to stand for 10 minutes.

Meanwhile, prepare the salad. Using a sharp paring knife, cut the peel, including all the white pith, from the grapefruit, then cut the segments free from the membranes. Cut the segments crossways into halves. Over a bowl, squeeze the juices from the membranes, then discard the membranes.

Cut the avocado into quarters lengthways, then remove the stone and peel. Cut the pieces lengthways into 5mm-thick slices, then arrange the slices on a large plate. Drizzle with the grapefruit juice and season with a pinch each of fine sea salt and white pepper.

Divide the watercress among 4 serving plates. Arrange the grapefruit sections on top. Add the oil and chopped tarragon to the shallot mixture and vigorously whisk to combine, then spoon the dressing over the salads. Sprinkle with the tarragon leaves and remaining pinch of white pepper, then scatter with a generous pinch or two of flaky coarse sea salt.

crushing peppercorns using elbow grease:

Whole peppercorns (black, white or red) coarsely crushed by hand yield larger flecks of the spice, which offer more robust bursts of flavour and more textural contrast to a dish than a coarse or fine grind from the mill. On a chopping board, press the base of a heavy frying pan against the whole peppercorns, rocking the pan back and forth to coarsely crush them, or carefully chop them with a chef's knife. A good pepper mill is great for a medium-coarse or fine grind, but you get a truer coarse crush when you do it by hand.

escarole salad with thinly sliced mushrooms and a marmalade-shallot vinaigrette

Using marmalade in a dressing allows you to put citrus, a little sweetness and the distinctive flavour of the preserve into a salad with one swoop of the spoon. If you're not already a marmalade aficionado, this salad might be a nice entry point. Marmalades range in flavour and texture, so your dressing will vary, depending on which sort you choose. Some are more sweet, others more bitter. Those marked 'thick cut' or 'coarse cut' include delicious pieces of toothsome rind in the mix. Frank Cooper's Vintage Oxford Marmalade is my favourite and the one that my mom brought me up on. It appeals to palates that prefer bitter to sweet. Use the marmalade you like best.

SERVES 4

VINAIGRETTE
50g thinly sliced shallots
**3½ tablespoons extra virgin
   olive oil**
**fine sea salt and freshly ground
   black pepper**
2 tablespoons orange marmalade
**1 teaspoon extra orange rind,
   coarsely chopped (optional)**
1 tablespoon white wine vinegar
1 teaspoon fresh lemon juice
1 tablespoon lukewarm water

**225g mixed mushrooms
   (see Box, page 39)**
**115g escarole or frisée, torn
   into bite-sized pieces**
115g baby spinach
flaky coarse sea salt

Make the base for the dressing by combining the shallots, oil, ⅛ teaspoon of fine sea salt and a generous pinch of black pepper in a small saucepan. Heat over a very low heat about for 10 minutes, stirring occasionally, until the shallots are very soft and just lightly golden. Transfer the mixture to a medium heatproof bowl, scraping every last drop of oil from the saucepan into the bowl, and leave to cool to room temperature.

Meanwhile, prepare the mushrooms. Trim the base of the button mushroom stems and very thinly slice both the tops and stems. If you are using enoki mushrooms, separate the clusters at their base into individual mushrooms or clusters of two or three.

When the shallots have cooled, add the marmalade plus 1 teaspoon of chopped orange rind, if using, the vinegar, lemon juice and ⅛ teaspoon each of fine sea salt and black pepper. Whisk well to combine, then whisk in the lukewarm water.

In a large serving bowl, combine the frisée and spinach. Add the dressing and toss. Season to taste with crushed flaky coarse sea salt and black pepper, then add the mushrooms and gently toss to combine. Garnish with extra orange rind from the marmalade, if desired.

tangle of radicchio and chicory with chives and blue cheese

In developing this recipe, I worked on three different versions of a classic blue cheese dressing. Creamy and delicious as they were, the mayo and other ingredients of the dressing seemed to overshadow the blue cheese. I wanted the cheese to be the star, so I reverted to a simple olive oil and vinegar dressing and sprinkled the cheese on top. The result? A tasty contrast of crunchy, slightly bitter salad greens and creamy, sweet blue cheese with a dressing that subtly makes its presence known. This salad loves a generous grinding of fresh black pepper, so if that's your style, season away.

SERVES 4

340g radicchio
340g chicory
1 tablespoon snipped fresh
   chives
2 tablespoons good-quality
   extra virgin olive oil
1 tablespoon red wine vinegar
fine sea salt and freshly ground
   black pepper
170g good-quality crumbly
   blue cheese, at room
   temperature (see Box)

Cut the radicchio in half lengthways. Cut out and discard the core, then cut the head crossways into 3mm-thick ribbons. Cut the chicory crossways on a slight diagonal, through the core, into 3mm-thick slices.

In a large bowl, combine the radicchio, chicory and chives. Add the oil, vinegar, and ½ teaspoon of salt and ¾ teaspoon of pepper. Toss to combine, then taste and adjust the seasoning, if necessary.

Mound the greens onto 4 serving plates, then crumble the blue cheese over the greens and season with more black pepper to taste.

frisée and herb salade au chapon

Props to my cousin Mark for inspiring me to create my own *salade au chapon,* a recipe he discovered in the British cookery writer Elizabeth David's book *French Provincial Cooking.* David explains that the recipe is great for those who like garlic but don't want to 'swallow whole hunks of the bulb'. She rubs raw garlic on toasted bread (*chapon*), which is tossed with the salad and then eaten at the end of the meal. My variation adds a mix of fresh herbs, a lemony dressing and a refashioned garlic technique. Gently poaching the garlic in oil softens both the bite and the bulb, and gives the oil a subtle garlic flavour. For the bread, I like a thick slice of *miche*, a rustic, slightly honeyed sourdough loaf with a dense, chewy crumb, dark crust and mild tang. Any good-quality, country-style bread can be substituted. I grill the bread on a cast-iron griddle pan, but it can also be toasted.

SERVES 4

DRESSING
2 tablespoons fresh lemon juice
1½ tablespoons finely chopped
   shallot
¼ teaspoon sugar
fine sea salt and freshly ground
   black pepper
4 tablespoons good-quality extra
   virgin olive oil

4 tablespoons extra virgin
   olive oil
4 garlic cloves, gently smashed
   and peeled
4 x 2cm-thick slices of country
   bread (e.g. pain de campagne),
   grilled or toasted
225g frisée
55g baby spinach
25g mixed herb leaves,
   e.g. mint, basil, coriander
   and chives
3 radishes, very thinly sliced
flaky coarse sea salt

Make the base for the dressing by stirring together the lemon juice, shallot, sugar, ½ teaspoon of fine sea salt and a generous pinch of black pepper in a medium bowl. Set aside.

In a small saucepan, combine the oil and garlic and gently heat over a very low heat for about 5 minutes until the oil is fragrant and the garlic is softened. (Tilt the pan, if necessary, to keep the garlic cloves submerged in the oil, and remove the pan from the heat from time to time to keep the garlic from colouring.) Remove the pan from the heat and whisk in ⅛ teaspoon of fine sea salt. Leave the mixture to stand for 10 minutes.

Put the grilled bread on a large plate and drizzle with the infused oil from the saucepan, then spread the garlic cloves on top. Tear the frisée into bite-sized pieces and combine in a bowl with the spinach, herbs and radishes.

Whisk the reserved dressing mixture while adding the good-quality oil in a slow and steady stream. Vigorously whisk to emulsify, then drizzle the dressing over the salad. Toss the salad to combine. Season with several pinches of flaky coarse sea salt and toss once more. Divide the salad among 4 serving plates. Tuck the breads among the greens.

garlic-poaching primer:

Poaching garlic in oil is best done in a tiny 0.5-litre saucepan. If you don't have one, I recommend adding this little size to your cookware collection. It is useful for heating up sauces or scalding milk for café con leche. You can also tilt a larger saucepan or frying pan to the side while gently heating the mixture, keeping the garlic submerged in the oil.

tender summer greens and nasturtiums with chive vinaigrette and fried capers

Edible flowers are beautiful and tasty. My first choice are nasturtiums but chive flowers or other edible flowers work just as well. If you don't have a garden or local farmers' market that stocks them, they may not be easy to come by. Luckily, this salad makes the grade with or without the flowers.

SERVES 4

VINAIGRETTE

2 tablespoons finely chopped
   chives
1 tablespoon finely chopped
   shallot
1½ tablespoons fresh
   lemon juice
½ teaspoon Dijon mustard
fine sea salt and freshly ground
   black pepper
4 tablespoons good-quality extra
   virgin olive oil

2 tablespoons capers, preferably
   salt-packed
1 large head red leaf lettuce or
   Bibb lettuce (see Box, page
   62), or 225g of any mix of
   tender greens
extra virgin olive oil for frying
1 small courgette, very thinly
   sliced into rounds
fine sea salt and freshly ground
   black pepper
55g nasturtiums (optional)

To make the dressing, place the chives, shallot, lemon juice, mustard, ⅛ teaspoon of salt and a generous pinch of pepper in a blender and combine. With the machine running, add the oil in a slow and steady stream until the dressing is well combined. Set aside.

Rinse the capers, soak in cold water for 10 minutes, then rinse again and pat dry. Remove the core from the lettuce and tear the leaves into bite-sized pieces.

Pour enough oil in a small frying pan to come about 3mm up the sides of the pan. Heat the oil over a medium-high heat until shimmering and fragrant. Add the capers and fry for about 1 minute, stirring often, until they crisp and open like flowerss. Using a slotted spoon, transfer to kitchen paper to drain.

In a large serving bowl, combine the lettuce, courgette and a pinch of salt and pepper. Add the dressing and gently but thoroughly toss to combine. Sprinkle with the nasturtiums, if using, and the capers.

regarding commercially packaged greens:

Though they're pre-washed, I like to give packaged greens a couple of good rinses in very cold water, as they can harbor harmful bacteria.

purslane and pumpkin seed salad à la grecque

Purslane offers a pleasing crunch, a lemony tang and a host of terrific nutrients, including impressive doses of vitamins A and C, calcium, iron and omega-3s. Look for this hearty summertime plant in farmers' markets or order it from specialist herb and salad suppliers (see Sources, page 170). Remove only the very thick stems, keeping the tasty tender ones in your bowl. When purslane is unavailable, try a mix of cress, lamb's lettuce and torn romaine.

SERVES 4

2 tablespoons fresh lemon juice
1½ tablespoons finely
  chopped shallot
fine sea salt
2 tablespoons good-quality
  extra virgin olive oil
dried oregano (see Box)
freshly ground black pepper
1 small cucumber
5 large radishes
40g Kalamata or mixed olives,
  stoned, coarsely chopped
340g purslane
1½ tablespoons finely
  chopped dill
135g feta cheese, crumbled
1 tablespoon roasted shelled
  pumpkin seeds (pepitas)

In a small bowl, stir together the lemon juice, shallot and ¼ teaspoon of fine sea salt then leave to stand for 10 minutes. Whisk in the oil, and add a generous pinch each of oregano and black pepper.

Peel the cucumber lengthways in zebra stripes. Quarter lengthways and then, using a mandoline, very thinly slice crossways. Slice the radishes very thinly crossways in the same way.

In a large bowl, combine the purslane, cucumber, olives, radishes and dill. Add the dressing and a pinch of salt. Gently but thoroughly toss to combine. Sprinkle the cheese and pumpkin seeds over the salad.

get me to the greek:

When it comes to dried oregano, go Greek. Greek oregano (sometimes called wild Greek oregano) is intensely aromatic and more robust-tasting than the average dried version. It's sometimes dried and sold on the stem, which is the type I tend to find in my Greek market. Crumble the herb into salad dressings, soups, stews and sauces. See Sources, page 170.

bibb lettuce with yogurt-chive dressing, smoked sea salt and cucumber

Smoked sea salt is nice for dipping radishes and cucumbers, and also in the dressing for this salad. If you don't have the salt, you can add smoky flavour by using a smoked cheese or fish in place of the feta. If you have a good cheesemonger or Italian food shop nearby, try fiore sardo, a firm Sardinian sheeps' milk cheese. A nice smoked Cheddar or smoked blue cheese also does the trick, or for a more filling salad, use smoked trout in place of the cheese. I'm not a fan of the waxy skin on conventional cucumbers, so I either peel those or buy unwaxed varieties.

SERVES 4

VINAIGRETTE
1 lemon
75ml 0% fat Greek yogurt
3 tablespoons mayonnaise
2 tablespoons finely chopped
   fresh chives
smoked sea salt
fine sea salt and freshly ground
   black pepper
40g mild sheeps' milk or goats'
   milk feta cheese, crumbled

2 heads Bibb lettuce (see Box)
1 cucumber, very thinly sliced

Make the dressing: Into a medium bowl, finely grate the zest from the lemon. Squeeze the lemon to make 2 teaspoons of juice and add it to the bowl, along with the yogurt, mayonnaise, 1 tablespoon of the chives, and ⅛ teaspoon each of the smoked sea salt, fine sea salt and black pepper. Whisk together to combine. Stir in the cheese.

Separate and arrange the lettuce leaves with the cucumber slices on 4 serving plates. Spoon the dressing over the lettuce and sprinkle with the remaining tablespoon of chives.

Bibb lettuce:

Bibb is a butterhead lettuce. Expect sweet, mild-tasting, tender leaves. Purchase heads that look fresh and crisp, avoiding leaves that are limp or have brown edges or spots. Since soft-leaved lettuces will keep for only up to 4 days, buy them as close to the time you are using them as possible.

rocket, cherries, marcona almonds and parmigiano-reggiano

Although inspired by golden cherries from the farmers' market, this pretty salad can be made with any sort of fresh or frozen cherries. Marcona almonds hail from Spain; their toasty, slightly sweet and salty flavour is a great match for the fruit. Toasted whole almonds and a few extra pinches of sea salt can be substituted.

SERVES 4

225g fresh cherries, stoned, or 390g frozen stoned cherries, thawed and drained

225g baby or wild rocket
55g Parmigiano-Reggiano or Grana Padano cheese, thinly shaved
18g Marcona almonds, coarsely chopped (see Sources, page 170)

3 tablespoons good-quality extra virgin olive oil
1 tablespoon white wine vinegar
flaky coarse sea salt and freshly ground black pepper

Cut the cherries in half lengthways and place in a large serving bowl. Add the rocket, cheese and almonds. Drizzle with the oil and vinegar, sprinkle with a few generous pinches of salt and season generously with black pepper. Toss to combine. Taste and adjust the seasoning, if necessary.

romaine salad with swiss cheese and anchovy croutons and a garlicky red wine vinaigrette

On this page and opposite are two anchovy lovers' salads you will find in the coming pages. I'm holding out hope that even my anchovy-averse readers might give them a try. A good anchovy, used properly, most definitely has the power to convert. The rustic croutons for this salad are fun to make – just tear the bread into irregular, bite-sized pieces.

SERVES 4 TO 6

1 head Romaine lettuce, trimmed and torn into bite-sized pieces
170g country bread (e.g. pain de campagne), cut into 2cm-thick slices then torn into irregualr pieces
85g freshly grated robust Swiss cheese, e.g. Emmental (use the medium holes of a box grater)
2 oil-packed anchovy fillets, finely chopped (see Box, opposite)

VINAIGRETTE
1 large garlic clove
½ teaspoon fine sea salt
3 tablespoons good-quality extra virgin olive oil
1 tablespoon red wine vinegar
freshly ground black pepper

Position a rack in the middle of the oven and preheat to 190°C/gas mark 5. Line a rimmed baking tray with baking paper. Put the lettuce into a large, wide serving bowl and set aside.

Spread the torn bread pieces onto the prepared baking tray and bake for 10 minutes, turning once halfway through.

Meanwhile, make the dressing. On a chopping board, slice the garlic clove, then mound the garlic together with the salt and, using both the blade and the flat side of a chef's knife, chop and scrape the mixture into a paste. Put the oil and vinegar into a bowl. Add the garlic paste and ¼ teaspoon of black pepper and vigorously whisk to combine.

Remove the tray of bread from the oven, sprinkle with three-quarters of the cheese and the anchovies (don't worry if some of the cheese and anchovy pieces land on the baking paper and not the bread – it'll all go into the salad eventually). Return the baking tray to the oven and bake for a further 2 minutes, until the cheese is melted and just lightly golden.

Remove the croutons from the oven. Working quickly but carefully, add the dressing to the bowl with the lettuce and toss to combine, then add the croutons and all the little bits of cheese and anchovy from the baking paper. Toss the salad well to combine all the elements.

Divide the salad among 4 serving plates and sprinkle with the remaining cheese. Season with additional black pepper, if desired.

bitter greens *alla romana*

If you've spent time in Rome, you might know about puntarelle: a feathery, pointy variety of chicory that grows wild in the Lazio region (puntarelle means 'little points'). The greens are less common outside Italy, but if and when you happen on them, seize the moment to make this delicious salad the classic way. Or, in place of the puntarelle, try curly endive, frisée or a combination of the two. The soaking of the greens in ice water mellows their bitter flavour. I like the mild spice and slightly herbal flavour of white pepper for this salad, but black pepper will work just as well.

SERVES 4

340g puntarelle, frisée
or curly endive,
or a combination

DRESSING
2 tablespoons white wine vinegar
4 oil-packed anchovy fillets
1 garlic clove, finely chopped
fine sea salt
freshly ground pepper,
preferably white
4 tablespoons extra virgin
olive oil

If using puntarelle or curly endive, trim the base then cut the leaves in half lengthways. If using frisée, trim the base and separate the leaves, tearing the larger leaves in half. Rinse the greens.

Fill a large bowl with ice and cold water, then submerge the greens in the ice water and leave them to soak for about 10 minutes until they curl up. Drain the greens, spin-dry and place in a large, wide bowl.

To make the dressing, purée the vinegar, anchovies, garlic and a pinch each of salt and pepper in a blender. With the machine running, add the oil in a slow and steady stream. Purée until well blended and fairly smooth.

Add the dressing to the greens and toss well to combine.

anchovies – undercover flavour agents:

Good-quality anchovies add a fantastic depth and savouriness unmatched by almost any other ingredient. I refer to them as 'undercover flavour agents' because they blend so seamlessly with other ingredients that their presence often goes unnoticed. Using anchovies in salad dressings is wonderful but they also provide punch in meaty stews and are tasty when mashed into unsalted butter for melting over roasted vegetables or spreading onto crostini. The nutrient-rich fish are packed with omega-3 fatty acids, which is an added bonus. The highest quality anchovies are packed in salt and need to be soaked, rinsed and sometimes filleted before using. Easier to use are oil-packed anchovy fillets.

oak leaf lettuce, fried green tomatoes and goats' cheese with a chimichurri vinaigrette

This salad is dressed with a mild, garlicky play on the spicy, vinegar-laced Argentine chimichurri sauce, which in its home country is commonly spooned over steak (the meat, in fact, makes a delicious addition here, if the mood strikes or leftovers are on hand). I love the elegant leaves of oak leaf lettuces, which are tender and mild. Torn butterheads, such as Bibb, or escarole lettuces make good substitutes. If green tomatoes are not available, try large tomatillos in their place.

SERVES 4

VINAIGRETTE
1½ tablespoons capers,
  preferably salt-packed
  (see Box, page 32)
6 tablespoons extra virgin olive
  oil, plus more for drizzling
1 tablespoon red wine vinegar
1 small garlic clove,
  very finely chopped
⅛ teaspoon chilli flakes
fine sea salt and freshly ground
  black pepper
6 tablespoons finely chopped
  flat-leaf parsley

115g fine cornmeal
fine sea salt and freshly ground
  black pepper
45g unbleached
  plain flour
1 medium egg beaten with
  2 tablespoons cold water
450g unripe green tomatoes, cut
  crossways into 1cm-thick slices
about 360ml olive oil for frying
115g green oak leaf lettuce
115g soft goats' cheese,
  crumbled
2 tablespoons chopped chives
flaky coarse sea salt

To make the vinaigrette, rinse the capers and then soak them in cold water for 10 minutes. Rinse again and coarsely chop. In a medium bowl, vigorously whisk together the oil, vinegar, garlic, chilli flakes, ⅛ teaspoon of salt and a generous pinch of black pepper. Add the parsley and capers and stir to combine well. Leave to stand at room temperature for at least 20 minutes or up to 3 hours if making ahead.

In a shallow bowl, stir together the cornmeal, ¾ teaspoon of salt and a generous pinch or two of black pepper. Place the flour and the egg mixture into 2 separate shallow bowls. Working with 1 slice at a time, dip the tomatoes in the flour, then in the egg mixture, then in the cornmeal, gently pressing to help the cornmeal adhere. Place the slices on a baking tray.

Line another baking tray with kitchen paper. Fill a large frying pan with 5mm of the oil and heat over a medium-high heat until shimmering but not smoking. In 2 batches, fry the tomatoes for 4–5 minutes on both sides until golden, turning once and reducing the heat if necessary. Transfer to the kitchen paper to drain.

Build the salads on 4 serving plates by layering a drizzle of vinaigrette, the lettuce, tomatoes, cheese, chives and more vinaigrette. Drizzle with the oil and sprinkle with a pinch of flaky coarse sea salt.

red kale caesar with mustard croutons and smoked trout

My first experience of eating raw kale was the flat- and tender-leafed Italian cavolo nero (black kale), also known as dinosaur or Tuscan kale. When my assistant Sue suggested I use Red Russian kale for this recipe, I was thrilled by the results. The red kale is equally delicious raw in a salad, and its purple stems and blue-green leaves are gorgeous. However, either black or red kale can be used here. In this salad I leave out anchovies to allow the trout to take centre stage. If not using trout, whisk one or two chopped anchovy fillets into the dressing.

SERVES 4

CROUTONS
3 tablespoons extra virgin
  olive oil
2 teaspoons wholegrain mustard
⅛ teaspoon fine sea salt
115g torn country bread

DRESSING
1 garlic clove
⅛ teaspoon fine sea salt
100g freshly grated Parmigiano-
  Reggiano
1 medium egg yolk
1 tablespoon plus 1½ teaspoons
  fresh lemon juice
1 teaspoon Dijon mustard
½ teaspoon Worcestershire
  sauce
cayenne pepper
¼ cup extra-virgin olive oil

450g Red Russian kale, stalks
  removed and coarsely chopped
225g skinless smoked trout
  fillets, flaked and pin bones
  removed

Preheat the oven to 180°C/gas mark 4. To make the croutons, line a rimmed baking tray with baking paper. In a large bowl, whisk together the oil, mustard and salt. Add the bread cubes and toss well. Spread the bread cubes out on the prepared baking tray in a single layer. Bake for about 15 minutes, stirring once, until lightly golden. Transfer the baking tray to a wire rack to allow the croutons to cool.

To make the dressing, slice the garlic clove on a chopping board, then mound the garlic together with the salt and, using both the blade and flat side of a chef's knife, chop and scrape the mixture into a paste. Place in a large bowl and add 25g of the cheese, the egg yolk, lemon juice, mustard, Worcestershire sauce and a pinch of cayenne pepper. Whisk vigorously while adding the oil in a slow and steady stream. Continue to whisk until the dressing is well combined.

Place the kale in the large bowl with the croutons and half of the trout and gently toss to coat. Divide the salad among 4 serving plates. Top with the remaining trout and cheese.

chapter three:

EGGS, POTATOES AND PASTA: CLASSICS REDUX

wild rocket, summer squash and asparagus with a fried egg and hot pickled peppers

Topping a big pile of greens with a breakfast-style egg makes a tasty and complete light brunch, lunch or dinner. The garlic here is used to flavour the oil for the fried eggs. I prefer to discard it once its job is done, but if you like an extra garlic punch, you can toss one or both of the cloves with the salad. Look for hot pickled jalapenos (red, yellow or green) in your local supermarket. They are also available in delis and farmers' markets, where you might find an oil-packed version (the oil is an extra treat – drizzle a little over the eggs in this salad just before serving).

SERVES 4

16 asparagus spears
1 medium summer squash
  (Patty Pan squash)
7 tablespoons extra virgin
  olive oil
fine sea salt and freshly ground
  black pepper
2 garlic cloves, gently smashed
  and peeled
4 medium eggs
225g baby or wild rocket
1 tablespoon balsamic vinegar
1 tablespoon chopped hot
  pickled peppers, plus more
  to taste

Trim the asparagus and cut in half crossways, then either halve or quarter the spears lengthways, depending on thickness. Cut the squash in half lengthways, then cut into 3mm pieces on the diagonal.

In a large non-stick frying pan, heat 2 tablespoons of the oil over a medium-high heat. Add the asparagus and season with a generous pinch of salt and pepper. Reduce the heat to medium and cook for about 8 minutes, stirring occasionally, until tender. Using tongs, transfer the asparagus to a large plate.

Add the squash to the pan and season with a pinch of salt and pepper. Cook for about 5 minutes, stirring occasionally, until tender. Using a slotted spoon, transfer the squash to the plate with the asparagus.

Add 2 tablespoons of the remaining oil and the garlic to the pan. Heat over a low heat for 5–7 minutes until tender, stirring frequently and occasionally tilting the pan to submerge the garlic in the hot oil (do not brown the garlic). Using a slotted spoon, remove and discard the garlic (see Box, page 59).

Crack the eggs into the pan. Season with a pinch of salt and pepper and cook over a medium-high heat for 2 minutes. Remove from the heat and leave the eggs to stand in the pan while you prepare the salad.

In a large bowl, combine the rocket, remaining 3 tablespoons of oil, vinegar, ⅛ teaspoon of salt and a generous pinch of pepper. Toss to combine, then taste and adjust the seasoning, if necessary.

Divide the rocket, asparagus and squash among 4 large serving plates. Arrange 1 egg on top of each serving of salad, then spoon over 1 tablespoon of the hot pickled peppers, or more to taste.

prawn and sweetcorn omelettes with an asian herb coleslaw

Here, pieces of fresh prawns, sweet onion and corn are cooked into a savoury omelette and a wispy coleslaw – delicately dressed with a touch of rice wine vinegar – provides a counterbalance of lively vegetables and bright herb flavours. If you can't find a Vidalia onion, a red onion will substitute nicely. If you have a mandoline, use the finest setting to julienne the vegetables.

SERVES 4

COLESLAW

2 medium carrots, julienned
1 small beetroot, julienned
3 medium radishes, julienned
2 spring onions, whites and
  greens, thinly sliced
2 tablespoons plus ½ teaspoon
  extra virgin olive oil
2 tablespoons rice wine vinegar
fine sea salt and freshly ground
  black pepper
2 tablespoons finely chopped
  coriander
1 medium cucumber, peeled
  and julienned
5g basil leaves, large leaves torn
5g mint leaves, large leaves torn

OMELETTE

7 medium eggs
150g medium or large prawns,
  peeled, deveined and
  coarsely chopped
8 tablespoons fresh or frozen
  sweetcorn kernels
1 Vidalia or red onion, finely
  chopped
2 tablespoons finely chopped
  coriander
1 teaspoon sugar
fine sea salt and freshly ground
  black pepper

In a large bowl, combine the carrots, beetroot, radishes and spring onions. Add 2 tablespoons of the oil, the rice wine vinegar, ¾ teaspoon of salt and a generous pinch of pepper. Toss the coleslaw to combine and set aside.

In a large bowl, beat the eggs until frothy, then add the prawns, sweetcorn, onion, 2 tablespoons of coriander, the sugar, ½ teaspoon of salt and a generous pinch of pepper. Whisk to combine.

In an 20cm non-stick frying pan, heat the remaining ½ teaspoon of oil over a medium-high heat until fragrant and shimmering. Stir together the egg mixture and ladle about a quarter of it into the pan, tilting the pan so that the egg mixture runs evenly to the edges. Reduce the heat to medium-low and cook for about 2 minutes until mostly dry all over, then loosen the edges of the egg with a spatula and fold it in half. Cook for a further 4–5 minutes until the prawns and eggs are cooked through, then slide onto a serving plate.

Without adding any more oil to the pan, repeat the process above to make 4 omelettes.

Just before you are ready to serve, add the remaining 2 tablespoons of coriander, the cucumber, basil and mint to the coleslaw, tossing to combine well. Taste and adjust the seasoning. Mound the coleslaw alongside the omelette on the serving plates and serve immediately.

to safely cut kernels from a corn cob:

Place a lightly dampened dishtowel, laid flat, under your cutting board, to prevent it from slipping. Using a sharp knife, cut a shucked ear of corn in half crosswise. Standing one half of the ear on your board, with the flat end facing down, cut the kernels from the ear in sections, close to the cob and in a downward motion.

greens, chorizo hash, lemon aïoli and boiled eggs

This family favourite was created over a weekend visit with cousins Mark and Katharine, a Sunday brunch response to Mark's Saturday dinner of slow-roasted Yucatán pork.

SERVES 4

HASH
450g small yellow- or red-
    skinned potatoes, about
    5cm in diameter
3½ tablespoons extra virgin
    olive oil
1 large onion, cut into
    5mm cubes
85g chorizo, cut into
    5mm cubes
fine sea salt

AIOLI
1 large garlic clove
fine sea salt
8 tablespoons mayonnaise
½ teaspoon lemon zest plus
    2 teaspoons fresh lemon juice
paprika, preferably smoked
    (see Sources, page 170)
cayenne pepper

SALAD
4 medium eggs
340g mixed greens
2½ tablespoons good-quality
    extra virgin olive oil, plus
    more for drizzling
1 tablespoon plus 1 teaspoon
    white wine vinegar
fine sea salt and freshly ground
    black pepper
8 radishes, cut into 5mm-thick
    wedges

To make the hash, place the potatoes in a large saucepan and cover with water. Add a pinch of salt, bring to the boil and cook for 10–15 minutes, depending on size, until tender. Drain the potatoes and leave to cool.

Meanwhile, make the aioli. Slice the garlic clove on a chopping board, then mound the garlic together with ⅛ teaspoon fine sea salt. Using both the blade and flat side of a chef's knife, chop and scrape the mixture into a paste. In a large bowl, whisk together the garlic paste with the mayonnaise, lemon zest and juice, and a generous pinch each of paprika and cayenne pepper. Set aside.

Cut the potatoes into 5mm cubes. In a large cast-iron or non-stick frying pan, heat 2 tablespoons of the oil over a medium-high heat until hot but not smoking. Add the onion, chorizo and ⅛ teaspoon salt. Reduce the heat to medium and cook for 10–12 minutes, stirring occasionally, until the onion is well softened. Using a slotted spoon (and leaving the oil in the pan), transfer the onion mixture to a bowl.

Return the frying pan to a medium heat. Add the remaining 1½ tablespoons of oil and heat until hot but not smoking. Add the potatoes in a single layer and cook for about 5 minutes, without stirring, until the bottoms are crisp. Cook for a further 5 minutes, stirring occasionally, until browned all over. Return the onion mixture to the pan, stir to combine, cover and remove from the heat.

To prepare the salad, pierce the rounded end of the eggs with a pin then place in a pan large enough to hold the eggs in a single layer. Add enough cold water to cover the eggs by about 3cm. Over a high heat, bring just to the boil then remove the pan from the heat. Tightly cover and leave to stand for 5 minutes for a gently boiled egg. Transfer the eggs to a bowl of ice water to stop the cooking process, and allow to cool completely. Gently tap the eggs all over to crack the shells then peel under cold running water.

In a large bowl, toss together the greens, oil, vinegar, ¼ teaspoon of salt and ⅛ teaspoon of pepper. Adjust the seasoning to taste. Divide the hash among 4 serving plates. Top with the salad and dollop with aïoli. Cut the eggs in half. Surround the salads with the eggs and radishes, drizzled with a little oil and sprinkled with salt and pepper.

shakshuka and a salad

Shakshuka is a delicious Middle Eastern and North African dish of eggs, gently poached in a rich tomato sauce fragrant with fresh chillies, onion and heady spices. Here, I serve it alongside greens tossed with a fresh lime dressing, which complement the dish well. If frisée is unavailable, substitute whatever greens look best at the market.

SERVES 4 TO 6

3 medium–large jalapeño
   peppers
4 tablespoons extra virgin
   olive oil
1 small onion, finely chopped
4 large garlic cloves, thinly
   sliced
1 teaspoon ground cumin
1 teaspoon paprika
2 x 400g tins good-quality
   crushed tomatoes, preferably
   San Marzano
fine sea salt
6 medium eggs

SALAD
115g frisée, torn
150–180g baby spinach
2 tablespoons fresh lime juice
2 tablespoons extra virgin
   olive oil
125g feta cheese, crumbled
1 tablespoon coarsely chopped
   coriander or flat-leaf parsley
warm wholewheat pitta bread
   for serving

Seed and finely chop the jalapeños, reserving some of the seeds if you like a spicy sauce.

In a 30cm frying pan, heat the oil over a medium-high heat. Add the jalapeños and onion, reduce the heat to medium-low and cook for about 12 minutes, stirring occasionally, until softened. Add the garlic, cumin, paprika and jalapeño seeds to taste, if using, and cook for a further 5 minutes, stirring frequently.

Add the crushed tomatoes, 120ml water and ¼ teaspoon of salt to the pan. Gently simmer the sauce for about 25 minutes, stirring occasionally, until thickened slightly.

Crack the eggs into the sauce one at a time and spaced apart from one another. Continue to cook, covered, for about 8 minutes until the yolks are just set.

While the eggs are cooking, prepare the salad. In a large bowl, toss together the frisée, spinach, lime juice, oil and ¼ teaspoon of salt. Divide the salad among the serving plates.

Uncover and baste the whites of the eggs with the sauce for about 2 minutes, to finish cooking, then remove from the heat.

Sprinkle the shakshuka with the cheese and coriander or parsley, then, using a large kitchen spoon, scoop onto the serving plates over and alongside the greens. Serve with warm pitta bread.

egg salad with lemon, capers and chives

The capers in this creamy egg salad take it from excellent to extraordinary. A plate of crisp cornichons and quick-pickled red onions bring additional brightness and beauty to the dish.

SERVES 4

6 medium eggs
2 tablespoons capers, preferably
   salt-packed
1 lemon
4 tablespoons mayonnaise
   (see Box, page 84)
10g finely chopped chives
fine sea salt and freshly ground
   black pepper
⅛ teaspoon piment d'Espelette
   or cayenne pepper (see
   Sources, page 170)

GARNISHES (OPTIONAL)
tender lettuce
toasted multigrain bread
quick pickled onions (see Black
   Bean salad, page 106)
cornichons

Pierce the rounded end of the eggs with a pin then place in a pan large enough to hold the eggs in a single layer. Add enough cold water to cover the eggs by 2.5cm. Over a high heat, bring just to the boil then remove the pan from the heat. Tightly cover leave to stand for 10 minutes.

Meanwhile, rinse the capers and soak them in cold water for 10 minutes. Rinse again and coarsely chop.

Transfer the cooked eggs to a bowl of ice water to stop the cooking process, and allow to cool completely in the water. Gently tap the eggs all over to crack the shells, then peel under cold running water. Coarsely chop and place in a large bowl.

Finely grate the zest of the lemon into the bowl, holding the zester close to capture any of the flavourful oils, and then squeeze the lemon to make 1½ teaspoons of juice. Add to the bowl, along with the mayonnaise, chives, capers, ¼ teaspoon of salt, black pepper and piment d'Espelette. Stir together gently to combine.

Serve with lettuce, bread, pickled onions, and cornichons, if desired.

purple potato salad with spring onions, tarragon and basil

This no-mayo French-style potato salad is a fantastic match for a plate of sausages, simple grilled fish or a whole meal of salads. The purple is very pretty, but any small potato variety can be used here. The key is to cut and toss the potatoes in their dressing while still warm – they take in the oil and vinegar dressing best that way.

SERVES 4 TO 6

900g small potatoes, such
   as small purple potatoes
   or fingerling
flaky coarse sea salt
4 tablespoons extra virgin
   olive oil
1 tablespoon white wine vinegar
freshly ground black pepper
2 spring onions, white and
   green parts, thinly sliced
   on a long diagonal
1 tablespoon finely chopped
   basil leaves
1 tablespoon coarsely chopped
   tarragon leaves

Place the potatoes in a large saucepan and add enough cold water to cover by about 5cm. Add a pinch of salt, bring to the boil and cook for about 10–15 minutes, depending on size, until tender. Drain and leave to cool completely.

While the potatoes are still warm, cut them into 1cm pieces and place in a bowl. Sprinkle with 1¾ teaspoons of salt, then add the oil, vinegar and ½ teaspoon of pepper. Gently stir to combine. Leave to stand for 5 minutes, then add the spring onions, basil and tarragon, and stir to combine. Serve the salad warm or at room temperature.

the not-so-ordinary potato:

The potato may seem quotidian, when in fact it is anything but that. This is evident at farmers' markets, where potatoes of many different colours, shapes and sizes can often be found. For potato salads, generally new potatoes and yellow- and red-skinned varieties work well, since all are good for boiling. Anya, Bintje, Désirée, Yukon Gold, Yellow Finn, Pink Fir Apple and purple potatoes are among the varieties you might happen on at a farmers' market or grow yourself. Although even the average supermarket potato makes a terrific salad, the less common varieties do wonders to break the boredom. Store potatoes in a cool, dry away from light. Refrigeration or temperatures under 7°C will convert the potato's starch to sugar, which does not taste good. And avoid potatoes with green skin, which may indicate the presence of the toxin solanine.

potato salad with za'atar and chives

A Lebanese blend of thyme (and sometimes other herbs), sesame seeds, sumac and salt, za'atar is a great seasoning for salads, roasted vegetables and grilled meat and fish. Here it lends its heady aroma and flavour to a deceptively simple potato salad.

SERVES 4

450g yellow- or red-skinned
  potatoes, about 5cm
  in diameter
70g mayonnaise (see Box)
3 tablespoons finely chopped
  chives
2 teaspoons za'atar
cayenne pepper
flaky coarse sea salt

Place the potatoes in a large saucepan and add enough cold water to cover by about 5cm. Add a pinch of salt, bring to the boil and cook for about 15 minutes, depending on size, until tender. Drain the potatoes and leave to stand until cool enough to handle.

Cut the potatoes into 5mm-thick wedges. Combine the potato wedges, mayonnaise, chives, za'atar and a generous pinch of cayenne pepper in a bowl. Sprinkle with ½ teaspoon of flaky coarse sea salt and gently toss to combine. Adjust the seasoning to taste.

mayo and greek yogurt choices:

I strongly advise against a reduced-fat, low-fat or 'light' mayonnaise. These seemingly 'healthier' versions of mayonnaise contain a host of synthetic ingredients and do not taste good either. When it comes to Greek yogurt, however, most good brands do not include additives. Full-fat, low-fat or fat-free Greek yogurt varieties can be used in any of my dressings. In general, checking ingredient labels on any food product that you purchase is good practice and will help ensure healthy, good-tasting dishes.

potato salad with melted leeks and blue cheese

'Slow and low' is a cheffy term used to describe a low-temperature, slow-cooking technique. The result is a delectable, extremely tender ingredient or dish that falls off the bone or melts in the mouth. Here, leeks are given this treatment, though the 'slow' is a mere 30 minutes, during which time the potatoes are prepared. The upshot? You get all the goodness of the 'slow and low' technique in a relatively short amount of time. And you enjoy a unique and tasty potato salad too.

SERVES 4 TO 6

1½ tablespoons unsalted butter
1½ tablespoons extra virgin
   olive oil
4 medium leeks, white and
   light green parts only, sliced
   crossways into 5mm rings,
   rinsed, drained and dried
fine sea salt and freshly ground
   black pepper
900g small potatoes,
   4–5cm in diameter
115g blue cheese, crumbled

In a large frying pan, heat the butter and oil over a medium-high heat until the butter is melted. Add the leeks and ¼ teaspoon each of salt and pepper, then stir to coat. Reduce the heat to medium-low and cook for about 30 minutes, stirring occasionally, until the leeks are very tender. Remove the pan from the heat and cover to keep warm.

Meanwhile, place the potatoes in a large saucepan and add enough cold water to cover by about 5cm. Add a pinch of salt, bring to the boil and cook for 10–15 minutes, depending on size, until tender. Drain the potatoes and leave to stand until cool enough to handle.

While the potatoes are still warm, quarter them or cut into eighths, depending on their size, and put the pieces in a large bowl. Add the leeks, cheese and ½ teaspoon of black pepper, then gently stir to combine. Serve the salad warm or at room temperature.

potato and sugar snap pea salad with garlic and parsley-lemon pesto

When sugar-snap peas show up at early summer markets, I love to make this vibrant salad. I might pair it with two or three salads from chapter one, depending on the length of my guest list, or serve it with a simple grilled fish.

SERVES 4 TO 6

900g small Yukon Gold potatoes
  (4–5cm in diameter)
fine sea salt and freshly ground
  black pepper
6 tablespoons extra virgin
  olive oil
2 large garlic cloves, gently
  smashed and peeled
1 lemon
150g sugar snap peas, strings
  removed
a handful of flat-leaf parsley
  leaves
a handful of basil leaves
35g pine nuts
25–30g freshly grated
  Parmigiano-Reggiano cheese,
  plus more for garnish
flaky coarse sea salt

Place the potatoes in a large saucepan and add enough cold water to cover by about 3cm. Add a pinch of salt then bring just to the boil. Reduce to a simmer and cook for 10–15 minutes, depending on size, until just tender. (The potatoes will continue to cook after draining so don't overcook them or they will break apart.)

While the potatoes are cooking, in a very small saucepan or frying pan, combine the oil, garlic and a pinch of fine sea salt. Heat gently over a very low heat for about 10 minutes, turning the garlic occasionally, until the oil is fragrant and the garlic is lightly golden. (If your pan is not small enough for the garlic to be submerged in the oil, tilt the pan frequently so that the garlic cooks evenly in the oil.) Transfer to a heatproof bowl and leave to cool completely.

Drain the potatoes and leave to stand until cool enough to handle. Cut the potatoes into 2cm pieces and put into a large bowl. While the potatoes are still warm, finely grate the zest of the lemon over them, then add a generous pinch each of fine sea salt and black pepper, and gently toss to combine. Set the potatoes aside to cool completely.

Cook the sugar-snap peas in a small saucepan of boiling salted water for about 2 minutes until crisp-tender. Drain, run under cold water to cool, then cut each pod crossways on a diagonal into 2 or 3 pieces.

Squeeze the lemon to make 2 teaspoons of juice. In a blender, combine the lemon juice, cooled oil mixture, parsley, basil, pine nuts, cheese, ½ teaspoon of fine sea salt and ¼ teaspoon of pepper. Purée until smooth.

Add the pesto and peas to the bowl with the potatoes and gently toss to combine. Transfer the salad to a serving bowl, sprinkle with a generous pinch or two each of crushed flaky coarse sea salt and black pepper. Garnish with a few shavings of cheese.

potato salad with charred poblano peppers, sweetcorn and crema

Steve and I are Mexican food devotees, and we're particularly fond of *rajas* – poblano chillies roasted over an open flame, then peeled and cut into strips. The mild smoky little strips are even tastier when tossed with Mexican crema, which is similar to crème fraîche or soured cream. One day I decided to fold the creamy peppers into a potato salad, with sweetcorn, onions, cumin and garlic, and created this new favourite dish.

SERVES 4 TO 6

900g small Yukon Gold potatoes
  (4–5cm in diameter)
fine sea salt and freshly ground
  black pepper
4 tablespoons extra virgin
  olive oil
3 corn on the cob, kernels
  removed
1 medium red onion, finely
  chopped
3 large garlic cloves, very
  thinly sliced
1 serrano chilli, thinly sliced
  crossways (with seeds)
2 large poblano chillies
4–5 tablespoons finely chopped
  coriander
4 tablespoons soured cream,
  preferably full fat
3 tablespoons plain yogurt,
  preferably whole milk
1½ tablespoons fresh lime juice
⅛ teaspoon ground cumin
flaky coarse sea salt

Place the potatoes in a large saucepan and add enough cold water to cover by about 3cm. Add a pinch of salt and bring just to the boil. Reduce to a simmer and cook for 10–15 minutes, depending on size, until just tender. (The potatoes will continue to cook after draining so don't overcook or they will break apart.)

Meanwhile, in a large frying pan, heat the oil over a medium-high heat until hot but not smoking. Add the sweetcorn and onion, reduce the heat to medium and cook, stirring frequently, for 8 minutes. Stir in the garlic and serrano chilli, including the seeds, and continue to cook for a further 2 minutes. Remove from the heat and leave to cool.

Drain the potatoes and leave to stand until cool enough to handle. Cut the potatoes into 2cm pieces and put in a large bowl. Season with a pinch each of fine sea salt and black pepper, and gently toss to combine. Set aside to cool completely.

Using tongs, char the poblano chillies over a gas flame, turning frequently, until the skin is blackened and blistered on all sides (or place them under a hot grill and cook until the skin is blistered). Transfer to a bowl, cover tightly with cling film and leave to stand for 15 minutes. Rub the skin off the peppers (do not rinse under water) and discard the core and seeds. Cut the peppers into 5mm pieces, then add to the bowl with the potatoes.

In a small bowl, stir together the coriander, soured cream, yogurt, lime juice and cumin. Add this crema and the sweetcorn mixture to the potatoes (be sure to scrape all of the oil and bits of garlic from the frying pan into the bowl). Gently toss to combine, then sprinkle with 1½–2 teaspoons of flaky coarse sea salt and gently toss once more. Adjust the seasoning to taste.

cracked potato salad with garlic and fresh herbs

Potatoes with crisped edges add a bit of texture to this salad, which is best served warm or at room temperature the day it is made. If making ahead on the day you are serving it, allow the salad to sit at room temperature, rather than in the fridge, for best texture.

SERVES 4 TO 6

900g new or red-skinned
   potatoes, about 5cm in
   diameter
flaky coarse sea salt
½ teaspoon paprika
coarsely cracked black pepper
⅛ teaspoon cayenne pepper
extra virgin olive oil for frying
a large handful of coriander,
   coarsely chopped
a large handful of mint, coarsely
   chopped

Place the potatoes in a large saucepan and add enough cold water to cover by about 3cm. Add a pinch of salt and bring just to the boil. Reduce to a simmer and cook for about 15 minutes, depending on size, until tender. (The potatoes will continue to cook after draining so don't overcook or they will break apart.)

Meanwhile, crush 1 teaspoon of flaky coarse sea salt into a small bowl. Add ¼ teaspoon of paprika, black pepper and cayenne pepper, and stir to combine.

Drain the potatoes and leave to stand until cool enough to handle. Place the warm potatoes on a clean work surface and, using the palm of your hand, very gently press each potato, just to slightly flatten and crack the skin.

Fill a large cast-iron or non-stick frying with enough oil to come 3mm up the sides of the pan. Heat the oil over a high heat until hot but not smoking. Fry the potatoes in batches for about 2 minutes on each side, seasoning them with the spice mixture, until the edges are golden and crisp. Transfer to a large bowl. While still hot, toss the potatoes with the coriander and mint. Serve the salad warm or at room temperature.

macaroni salad with yogurt, dill and pickles

My mother made a variation of this pasta salad throughout our childhood. She would pack it for a trip to the beach or serve it alongside her sweet, sticky barbecued ribs for outdoor summer suppers. It's still one of my most favourite dishes. I love the play of fresh dill and crisp celery against the sweet tang of the lemon, pickles and creamy mayo background. Be sure to cook your pasta al dente; a firm textured pasta is always much more appealing and more delicious than a mushy one and – in any pasta dish – will make the difference between a good and great result.

SERVES 6 TO 8

450g gemelli, penne, ziti or
   mezzi rigatoni
2 tablespoons extra virgin
   olive oil
240ml mayonnaise
120ml 0% fat Greek-style
   yogurt
120ml whole or semi-skilled
   milk
fine sea salt and freshly ground
   black pepper
1 large lemon
500g cherry or grape tomatoes,
   quartered
about 5 medium dill pickles
   (or gherkins), diced
70g very thinly sliced spring
   onion, white and green parts
a handful of dill, finely chopped
2 celery stalks, finely diced

Bring a large pan of salted water to the boil. Cook the pasta in the boiling water until al dente, then drain without rinsing. Transfer to a rimmed baking tray set on a wire rack. Drizzle the pasta with the oil and leave to cool to room temperature, about 5 minutes.

Meanwhile, in your largest mixing bowl, whisk together the mayonnaise, yogurt, milk, ¾ teaspoon of fine sea salt and ½ teaspoon of black pepper. Finely zest the lemon into the bowl, holding the zester close so that you capture the flavourful oil. Squeeze the lemon to make 1 tablespoon of juice, then add to the mixture. Whisk together to make the dressing.

Add the pasta, tomatoes, pickles, spring onion, dill and celery to the dressing. Stir well to combine. Serve the salad at room temperature.

cooking pasta to al dente and other pasta cooking tips:

For best pasta results, cook pasta in a large, heavy-based pan of well-salted boiling water (the salt seasons both the pasta and its cooking water, which is terrific as the flavourful starchy liquid is sometimes used to moisten a sauce). Stir the pasta when it is first added to the boiling water and occasionally during cooking to prevent sticking. Al dente means 'to the tooth'; the pasta should have a bite and be slightly opaque in the centre. Pasta continues to cook for a while after it has been drained, especially when it is cooling on a tray for pasta salads, so begin checking for doneness 1–2 minutes before the suggested time on the box and do not be afraid to drain your pasta too early. Do not rinse cooked pasta or you will rinse away most of its flavour.

wholewheat pasta salad with shredded roast chicken, capers, marjoram and ricotta salata

For those of you who enjoyed recipes using roast chicken in pastas and other dishes from my cookbook *The Perfectly Roasted Chicken*, here's a new one to add to the mix. This is a nice salad to bring to a picnic or to serve as a made-ahead summer lunch or dinner. I like the toothsome and earthy qualities of wholewheat pasta, though ordinary pasta can be used. Try fresh oregano in place of marjoram, if you like.

SERVES 6 TO 8

450g wholewheat pasta shells
fine sea salt and freshly ground
   black pepper 40g capers,
   preferably salt-packed (see
   Box, page 32)
8 tablespoons extra virgin olive
   oil, plus more for drizzling
2 large garlic cloves, gently
   smashed and peeled
120ml 0% fat Greek-style
   yogurt
3 tablespoons finely chopped
   marjoram
1 large or 2 small lemons
450g shredded roast chicken
   (see Box)
170g ricotta salata or feta
   cheese, crumbled

Bring a large pan of salted water to the boil, then cook the pasta until al dente. Meanwhile, rinse the capers and soak in cold water for 10 minutes. Rinse again, then coarsely chop.

In a small saucepan, combine 6 tablespoons of the oil and the garlic. Gently warm over a very low heat for about 5 minutes, lifting the pan and swirling the garlic occasionally (do not let it brown), until the garlic is softened and the oil is very fragrant. Transfer to a very large bowl and set aside to cool to room temperature.

Remove and discard the garlic from the oil, then add the capers, yogurt and 2 tablespoons of the marjoram. Finely zest the lemon into the bowl, holding the zester close so that you capture the flavourful oil. Squeeze the lemon to make 1 tablespoon of juice, then add to the mixture. Stir the dressing to combine.

Drain the pasta without rinsing and transfer to a rimmed baking tray set on a wire rack. Drizzle with 2 tablespoons of oil and sprinkle with ¼ teaspoon each of the salt and pepper. Stir to evenly coat and leave to cool completely, about 10 minutes.

Add the pasta, chicken and cheese to the bowl with the dressing, and toss to combine. Taste and adjust the seasoning. Transfer to a serving bowl, sprinkle with the remaining 1 tablespoon of marjoram and drizzle with the remaining oil. Serve the salad at room temperature.

choosing a rotisserie bird:

This recipe is a great way of using surplus roast chicken, or you can buy a rotisserie chicken. If purchasing the latter, make sure it is a good-quality bird (they can be dry and disappointing) that has been seasoned with salt and pepper while roasting (herbs and other seasonings are fine too). Unseasoned birds tend to be bland even if seasoned later, once you bring them home.

warm orzo salad with sweet crab, shiitake mushrooms, sweetcorn and crème fraîche

This delicate salad is delicious on its own, but I like it best alongside a pile of crisp lettuces dressed with a lemony vinaigrette. Frisée and Herb Salade au Chapon (page 59) makes an especially good match, or you can toss the dressing from that recipe with any sort of greens. A little plate of ribs or grilled meat of any kind nicely rounds out the meal if you are hosting a summer barbeque.

SERVES 4 TO 6

270g orzo pasta
5 tablespoons extra virgin
  olive oil
2 corn on the cob, kernels
  removed
2 tablespoons finely chopped
  shallot
fine sea salt and freshly ground
  white pepper
340g shiitake mushrooms,
  stemmed and cut into 3mm-
  thick slices (see Box, page 39)
a small bunch of flat-leaf parsley,
  finely chopped
225g white crab meat,
  picked over
115ml crème fraîche
15g finely chopped chives
3 tablespoons thinly sliced
  basil leaves
cayenne pepper

Bring a large pan of salted water to the boil. Add the orzo and cook until al dente. Drain the orzo and spread on a rimmed tray set on a wire rack to cool.

In a large non-stick frying pan, heat 2 tablespoons of the oil over a medium-high heat. Add the sweetcorn, shallot, ½ teaspoon of salt and ¼ teaspoon of white pepper. Reduce the heat to medium-low and cook for about 5 minutes, stirring occasionally, until the corn is crisp-tender. Add the mushrooms and parsley. Continue to cook for a further 5 minutes, stirring frequently, until the mushrooms are wilted and tender. Remove the pan from the heat.

Transfer the orzo to a large bowl and add the remaining 3 tablespoons of oil, the mushroom mixture, crab meat, crème fraîche, chives, basil, ¾ teaspoon of salt and a pinch or two of cayenne pepper. Stir the salad to combine, then adjust the seasoning to taste. Serve at room temperature.

muffaletta pasta salad

The *muffaletta* is a crazy-delicious New Orleans sandwich layered high with slices of salumi (Italian cured meats such as mortadella, prosciutto and salami), provolone or Emmental cheese, and a piquant 'salad' comprised of juicy chopped olives, olive oil and a variety of chopped vegetables that might include capers, friggitelli peppers and celery. Thick slices of sesame-seed bread sandwich all the good stuff together, then, wrapped tightly in cling film, the mighty mound 'rests' to allow its flavours to mingle. In this variation the meats and cheese are julienned, a twist-shaped pasta catches all the good bits nicely, and if allowed to sit for an hour or (better still) a day, the salad, like its namesake sandwich, is even better. Although a long ingredient list may seem daunting, most are store cupboard or deli items.

SERVES 6 TO 8

1 tablespoon salt-packed capers (see Box, page 32)

2 large celery stalks, coarsely chopped

a handful of flat-leaf parsley, coarsely chopped

65g pimento-stuffed green olives

a handful of fresh basil, coarsely chopped

35g black olives, stoned

2 friggitelli (mild) peppers, stems trimmed

1 large garlic clove, peeled

freshly ground black pepper and fine sea salt

⅛ teaspoon chilli flakes

4 tablespoons extra virgin olive oil

1 tablespoon red wine vinegar

225g thinly sliced mixed cold cuts, including mortadella, prosciutto and salami

450g fusilli pasta

150g Emmental cheese, grated

Bring a large pan of salted water to the boil.

Rinse the capers, then soak in cold water for 10 minutes. Rinse again, then place in a food processor with the celery, parsley, green olives, basil, black olives, friggitelli, garlic, ⅓ teaspoon of black pepper, ¼ teaspoon of salt and the chilli flakes. Purée until finely chopped. Add the oil and vinegar and purée to combine.

Working with about a quarter of the meats at a time, roll the slices and thinly slice into julienne. Unroll and separate the strands.

Add the pasta to the pan of boiling salted water and cook until al dente, then drain and transfer to a large serving bowl. While the pasta is hot, add the purée and the meats and sesame seeds. Toss to combine well. In three batches, add the cheese, tossing to combine between additions. Serve the salad warm or at room temperature.

israeli couscous salad with merguez sausage and mustard leaves

The toothsome, tender pearls of Israeli couscous, also known as giant couscous, are larger and more pasta-like than the much finer grains of their Moroccan counterpart; both varieties work in salads. Merguez sausage is traditionally made with lamb, but it is also prepared with beef or a mixture of the two. I tend to opt for the rich gaminess of the lamb variety, but any good-quality version is delicious. Look for merguez in speciality butcher's shops, farmers' markets and online. Israeli couscous can be found at most good supermarkets.

1 bunch of mustard leaves
   (285–340g)
45g sultanas
28g flat-leaf parsley, coarsely
   chopped
20g sliced almonds
1 large garlic clove, coarsely
   chopped
3½ tablespoons extra virgin
   olive oil
250g Israeli or giant couscous
fine sea salt
410–480ml vegetable or
   chicken stock
285g merguez sausage
85–90g finely chopped onion
freshly ground black pepper
10g finely chopped mint

Cut the centre rib and stem from the mustard greens and slice the leaves into 5mm-wide strips. Submerge in a large bowl of cold water to rinse, then transfer to another bowl, leaving moisture on the leaves for cooking. Set aside.

Soak the sultanas in hot water for 15 minutes, then drain. Mound the sultanas with the parsley, almonds and garlic in the centre of a chopping board and finely chop together. Transfer to a small bowl and set aside.

In a medium heavy-based saucepan, heat 1 tablespoon of oil over a medium heat. Add the couscous and a pinch of salt and cook for about 5 minutes, stirring occasionally, until golden. Add 410ml stock and bring to the boil. Reduce the heat to medium-low, cover and simmer for about 10 minutes, until the liquid is absorbed and the couscous is tender, adding more stock by tablespoonfuls if too dry. Spread the cooked couscous on a rimmed baking tray set on a wire rack and leave to cool

Meanwhile, heat a large non-stick frying pan over a medium-high heat. Add the sausage, reduce the heat to medium and cook for about 15 minutes, turning occasionally, until cooked through. Transfer to a chopping board. Pour off and discard the pan juices from the pan but do not wipe clean.

Return the frying pan to a medium heat and add 1½ tablespoons of oil. Heat the oil until hot but not smoking, then add the onion and a generous pinch each of salt and pepper. Reduce the heat to low and cook for about 10 minutes, stirring frequently, until the onion is softened and sweet. Using a rubber spatula, scrape the onion and the oil from the pan over the couscous.

Return the frying pan to a medium-high heat and add the remaining tablespoon of oil. Heat until hot but not smoking, then add the mustard greens. Reduce the heat to medium and cook for 8–10 minutes, stirring frequently, until tender. Add the reserved sultana mixture and a generous pinch each of salt and pepper. Cook, stirring constantly, for a further 1–2 minutes. Transfer to a large plate and leave to cool to room temperature, about 10 minutes.

Meanwhile, transfer the couscous to a large mixing bowl. Thinly slice the sausages and add to the bowl. Add the cooled greens and mint, and stir to combine. Season generously with salt and pepper.

chapter four:

A BOUNTY OF BEANS, GRAINS AND LEGUMES

freekeh salad with broad beans, grilled asparagus and roasted lemon

Earthy, slightly smoky, nutty and nutrient-rich, freekeh (pronounced free-ka) is one of my favourite grains for salads and side dishes. Look for it in Middle Eastern food shops and online. If freekeh is unavailable, try barley or wholewheat pasta. Peas can be used in place of broad beans. Roasting lemons is one of my best-loved techniques. The slightly charred slices hint at preserved lemons, though they are a little less intense.

SERVES 4 TO 6

255g freekeh (see Sources, page 170)
fine sea salt
7 tablespoons extra virgin olive oil
450g asparagus, trimmed
freshly ground black pepper
1 lemon
1 large red onion, finely chopped
2 garlic cloves, thinly sliced
½ teaspoon fennel seeds, finely ground (see Box, opposite)
250g shelled fresh broad beans (about 1kg in pods) or frozen broad beans, thawed
Aleppo pepper (see Sources, page 170) or cayenne pepper

Place a rack in the middle of the oven and preheat to 190°C/gas mark 5. Line a rimmed baking tray with baking paper.

In a large saucepan, combine 950ml of water, the freekeh, 1 teaspoon of salt and 1 tablespoon of oil. Bring to the boil over a high heat, then reduce to a gentle simmer, cover and cook for 40–45 minutes, until the freekeh is tender but still toothsome and the water is mostly absorbed.

Meanwhile, grill the asparagus for 10–12 minutes, depending on thickness, until crisp-tender. Transfer to a plate and, while hot, drizzle the asparagus with 1 tablespoon of oil and season generously with salt and black pepper.

Rinse and dry the lemon, then trim the ends and cut the lemon crossways into 3mm-thick rounds. Remove and discard any pips. Lay the lemon slices in a single layer on the prepared baking tray, then drizzle with 2 tablespoons of oil and season with ¼ teaspoon each of salt and black pepper.

Roast the lemon slices for 18–24 minutes until golden, rotating the tray once halfway through and transferring any quick-browning slices to a plate as they're ready. (Keep a careful eye on the slices – the ones on the outer edges of the tray will brown quicker than those in the centre; you want a nice golden colour, but watch that the slices don't burn, especially towards the end of cooking.) Transfer the roasted slices to a plate to cool, then finely chop.

When the freekeh is ready, drain excess water, then transfer to a large bowl.

Meanwhile, heat the remaining 3 tablespoons of oil in a large non-stick frying pan over a medium-high heat. Add the onion, garlic, fennel seeds and a generous pinch of salt. Reduce the heat to medium-low and gently cook for about 10 minutes, stirring occasionally, until the onion is tender. Add the chopped lemon and stir to combine. Cook for a further 2 minutes, then remove the pan from the heat and set aside.

Meanwhile, bring a medium saucepan of salted water
to the boil and cook the broad beans in the boiling salted
water for 2 minutes. Drain and run under cold water
to cool, then peel if using fresh beans. Add the beans
and the onion mixture to the bowl with the freekeh.
Cut the asparagus into 2.5cm lengths and add it as well.

Add ¼ teaspoon of salt and 1–2 teaspoons of Aleppo
pepper, or a pinch of cayenne, then stir to combine.
Adjust the seasoning to taste.

grinding whole spices:

I like to grind my own fennel seeds and other whole
spices as needed, using a spice grinder or a retired
coffee grinder (keep the grinder for spices in a
separate cabinet from the one used for coffee so
as not to confuse). A mortar and pestle can also
be used. Whole seeds freshly ground offer a more
vibrant flavour than the pre-ground versions. At a pinch,
pre-ground seeds will certainly do.

panzanella di farro (tuscan bread salad with spelt grains)

Although tomatoes and basil are a must, feel free to vary the other vegetables in this no-bread panzanella. Celery, asparagus and sugar-snap peas can be added or used instead. Grilling the green beans adds a toasty flavour; it's easy on a griddle pan or when you're firing up the barbecue for a larger meal. If the extra step is too much, just stick to blanching the beans instead.

SERVES 4 TO 6

340g cherry or grape tomatoes, halved
fine sea salt
1 large corn on the cob, husk removed
225g green beans, trimmed
6 tablespoons good-quality extra virgin olive oil
200g farro (see Sources, page 170)
1 large garlic clove
3 tablespoons red wine vinegar
finely ground black pepper
1 small cucumber, peeled and sliced into half moons
a small bunch of basil, large leaves torn
4 medium radishes, halved and very thinly sliced
3 spring onions, white and green parts, thinly sliced

Bring a large saucepan of salted water to a boil.

In a large serving bowl, toss together the tomatoes and ½ teaspoon of salt. Set aside.

Cook the corn on the cob and the green beans together in the boiling water for 3 minutes. Using tongs, transfer the corn to a chopping board. Continue to cook the green beans for a further 1–2 minutes until crisp-tender. Using tongs, transfer the beans to a colander to drain, pat dry and place in a medium bowl (reserve the pan of water). Add 1 tablespoon of the oil and toss to combine.

Cook the farro for 18–20 minutes in the water that you used for the corn and beans, stirring occasionally, until tender but still firm to the bite.

Meanwhile, heat a griddle pan over a medium-high heat. Grill the green beans for 4–5 minutes until golden on both sides. Transfer to a plate and season with a generous pinch of salt and pepper. Leave the beans to cool, then cut into 2.5cm lengths. Cut the kernels off the corn on the cob.

Slice the garlic clove on a chopping board, then mound the garlic together with ½ teaspoon salt and, using both the blade and the flat side of a chef's knife, chop and scrape the mixture into a paste. In a medium bowl, combine the remaining 5 tablespoons of oil and the vinegar. Add the garlic paste and ¼ teaspoon of pepper, and vigorously whisk the dressing to combine.

Drain the farro, then spread it on a rimmed baking tray set over a wire rack to cool for 5–10 minutes.

When the farro is cool, whisk together the dressing and add it to the tomatoes, along with the farro, green beans, sweetcorn, cucumber, basil, radishes, spring onions, ¾ teaspoon of black pepper and ¼ teaspoon of salt. Toss the salad to combine well.

warm farro and sweet onion salad with wilted escarole and fontina

Fontina is a sweet, nutty cheese with a supple texture that melts just the perfect amount over this hearty warm grain salad. Although you can purchase Danish, French, Swedish and US-made versions of the cheese, I recommend spending money on the robust, genuine Italian item from the western Alps region, the Val d'Aosta, when it's available. Torn Bibb leaves can be substituted for escarole, if you like.

SERVES 4

- 2 medium onions, cut into 1cm-thick wedges
- 3½ tablespoons extra virgin olive oil
- ½ teaspoon dried thyme
- fine sea salt and freshly ground black pepper
- 155–170g farro
- 1½ tablespoons balsamic vinegar
- 1 large garlic clove, gently smashed and peeled
- 1 head escarole (225–340g)
- 115g Fontina cheese, cut into 5mm cubes
- flaky coarse sea salt

Place a rack in the middle of the oven and preheat to 200°C/gas mark 6. Line a rimmed baking tray with baking paper.

In a bowl, gently toss together the onions, 1½ tablespoons of oil, the thyme, ¼ teaspoon of fine sea salt and ⅛ teaspoon of pepper. Arrange the onions in a single layer on the prepared baking tray, then, using a rubber spatula, scrape the oil and spices from the bowl on top of the onions. Roast the onions for about 30 minutes, turning and flipping them once halfway through, until golden and tender.

Meanwhile, bring a large saucepan of salted water to the boil. Add the farro and cook for about 18 minutes until tender. Drain and transfer to a large bowl. Add the roasted onions and vinegar and gently toss to combine. Set aside.

In a large frying pan, combine the remaining 2 tablespoons of oil, the garlic and ¼ teaspoon of fine sea salt. Heat over a low heat for about 3 minutes, until the oil begins to bubble. Add the escarole, increase the heat to medium-high, and cook for about 3 minutes, stirring frequently, until the greens are wilted. Remove the pan from the heat and discard the garlic.

Separate and tear the leaves of the escarole and divide among 4 serving plates. Top with the farro mixture, then the cheese. Sprinkle with flaky coarse sea salt to taste.

tabbouleh with fennel and grapes

Tabbouleh is one of my favourite salads, especially when seasoned with copious amounts of freshly chopped herbs. This one gets a bit of extra texture and a little sweetness from the addition of fresh fennel and thinly sliced grapes.

SERVES 4 TO 6

170g medium or coarse
  bulgur wheat
1 medium fennel bulb
  with fronds
1 medium cucumber
200g red or green grapes,
  or a mixture
a small handful of mint, finely
  chopped, plus extra leaves
  for garnish
a small handful of flat-leaf
  parsley, finely chopped
4 spring onions, white and green
  parts, thinly sliced
6 tablespoons good-quality
  extra virgin olive oil
3 tablespoons fresh lemon juice
1¼ teaspoons fine sea salt
½ teaspoon ground fennel seeds
  (see Box, page 101)

Put the bulgur wheat in a large bowl. Add 360ml of boiling water, then cover the bowl tightly with cling film and leave to stand for about 20 minutes, until the bulgur wheat is tender but still quite firm to the bite.

Meanwhile, prepare the salad. Finely chop the fennel bulb and fronds, keeping them separate. Peel and cut the cucumber into 5mm cubes, leaving the seeds in. Slice the grapes thinly crossways.

Drain the bulgur wheat in a sieve to extract any remaining water, then spread on a baking tray set on a wire rack to cool for 5 minutes. Transfer to a large bowl.

Add the fennel, all but 2 tablespoons of its fronds, the cucumber, all but 50g of the grapes, the mint, parsley, spring onions, oil, lemon juice, salt and fennel seeds. Stir to combine.

Transfer the tabbouleh to a serving bowl and garnish with the reserved grapes, fennel fronds and mint leaves.

white bean salad with fresh mint and sumac-honey vinaigrette

This citrusy salad is one I like to make an hour or two or even a day ahead, which allows the flavours to blend further. If you do get a head start, bring the dish to room temperature before serving. Sumac is a Middle Eastern spice that lends a pleasingly astringent taste and an added lemony tang here. If you're new to it, you'll find it's delicious in rice and vegetable dishes and great as a seasoning for grilled or roasted meats and fish.

SERVES 4 TO 6

55g finely chopped red onion
5 tablespoons fresh lemon juice
½ teaspoon fine sea salt
¼ teaspoon freshly ground
   black pepper
2 x 410g tins cannellini or
   butter beans, drained and
   rinsed (or 450g soaked and
   cooked dried beans)
4 tablspoons extra virgin
   olive oil
4 tablespoons finely chopped
   mint
2 teaspoons honey
½ teaspoon sumac
cayenne pepper

Stir together the onion, lemon juice, salt and black pepper in a small bowl, then leave the mixture to stand for 15 minutes.

Rinse and drain the beans, then transfer to a large bowl.

Gently heat the oil in a small saucepan over a low heat, until warmed through. Add the lemon juice mixture and the warm oil to the beans, then add the mint, honey, sumac and a generous pinch of cayenne pepper. Gently toss together to combine.

If you have time, leave the salad to stand at room temperature for 1 hour, or cover and refrigerate overnight, then bring to room temperature before serving.

loving the leftovers:

Pasta, grain, bean and rice salads, as well as 'sturdy-ingredient' salads, such as many slaws, fennel and celery root salads, keep well (refrigerated) for days and make great leftovers.

black bean salad with prawns and pickled onions

Although I'm generally an advocate of cooking with dried beans and legumes – which are easy to cook, but require extra time for soaking and boiling – I've found that good-quality tinned beans work well here.

SERVES 4

PICKLED ONIONS
180ml distilled white vinegar
3 tablespoons sugar
1 bay leaf
10 whole black peppercorns
3 juniper berries
⅛ teaspoon fine sea salt
⅛ teaspoon chilli flakes

⅛ teaspoon whole cumin seeds
1 large red onion, thinly sliced crossways and separated into rings

2 x 425g tins black beans, rinsed and drained
2 spring onions, white and green parts, thinly sliced

4 tablespoons finely chopped coriander, plus more for garnish (optional)
6 tablspoons extra virgin olive oil
3 tablespoons fresh lime juice
fine sea salt
16 large prawns, peeled and deveined
1 large garlic clove, thinly sliced
100g feta cheese

Place all of the pickled onion ingredients, except the onion, in a medium heavy-based frying pan and bring to the boil, whisking to dissolve the sugar. Add the onion, reduce to a simmer and cook, gently stirring, for 1 minute. Transfer to a heatproof bowl and leave to cool for about 30 minutes.

In a large serving bowl, stir together the beans, spring onions, coriander, 4 tablspoons of oil, the lime juice and ¼ teaspoon of salt. Set aside.

Heat the remaining 2 tablespoons of oil in a large frying pan over a medium-high heat until hot but not smoking. Add the prawns and a generous pinch of salt and cook for 1 minute. Add the garlic and cook for 1–2 minutes, stirring occasionally, until the prawns are cooked through. Transfer to the serving bowl and toss. Crumble the cheese over the salad and sprinkle with extra coriander, if desired. Remove the pickled onions from their pickling liquid and serve on the side.

lentil and beet salad with spring onions and basil

In this colourful, earthy salad, beetroot leaves and stems are cooked and added along with the beets themselves for additional flavour and texture, and an extra boost of vitamins, minerals and antioxidants. When shopping for lentils, look for small ones, such as French Puy, Spanish pardina or Italian Castelluccio or Colfiorito. These types are firm-tender, not mushy, and hold their shape once cooked.

SERVES 6

4 small–medium beetroots,
  with leaves and stems
250–300g small green or brown
  lentils, sorted to remove debris
  and rinsed
1 celery stalk, cut crossways into
  3 pieces
2 garlic cloves, gently smashed
  and peeled
fine sea salt
8 tablespoons extra virgin
  olive oil
freshly ground black pepper
2 large spring onions, thinly
  sliced on a long diagonal
6–8 basil leaves, thinly sliced
2 tablespoons fresh lemon juice

Place a rack in the middle of the oven and preheat to 200°C/gas mark 6. Trim the beetroots, leaving on about 5mm of the stems. Set aside the trimmed stems and leaves.

Put the beetroots in a baking dish and add enough water to come about 1cm up the sides. Cover the dish tightly with foil and roast the beets for 45 minutes–1 hour, depending on their size, until tender right through when pierced with a knife or a skewer.

Meanwhile, place the lentils, celery, 1 garlic clove and ½ teaspoon of salt in a medium saucepan and add 1 litre of water. Bring the mixture just to the boil, then reduce to a gentle simmer and cook for 30–40 minutes until tender, stirring occasionally and adding water if necessary to keep the lentils covered.

While the beetroots and lentils are cooking, finely chop the beet stems and coarsely chop the leaves. Rinse well, leaving moisture on the greens for cooking. In a large frying pan, heat 1 tablespoon of the oil over a medium-high heat. Add the remaining garlic clove, the beet stems and leaves and a generous pinch of salt and pepper. Reduce the heat to medium and cook for about 10 minutes, stirring occasionally, until the greens are tender. Remove the pan from the heat and discard the garlic.

Drain the lentils and discard the celery and garlic. Remove the beets from the oven and uncover. When cool enough to handle, peel the beets (the skins will easily slip off) and cut into small wedges or cubes.

In a large bowl, combine the beet-green mixture, roasted beets, lentils, remaining 7 tablespoons of oil, spring onions, basil, lemon juice, 1 teaspoon of salt and ¼ teaspoon of pepper. Gently toss to combine.

lentils, grilled radicchio and chorizo

My brother Jason is another professional and wonderful cook in our family. He suggested the addition of grilled radicchio when I told him about this salad, and it turned out to be the missing link. I like to use two types of extra virgin olive oil here, one to cook with and a more robust-tasting oil to finish the salad, but just one oil can be used if you prefer. To turn this salad into a hearty little meal, try a poached or fried egg on top.

SERVES 4

155g cooking chorizo (see Sources, page 170)
4½ tablespoons extra virgin olive oil
30g finely chopped onion
3 large celery stalks, finely diced, plus 3 tablespoons coarsely chopped celery leaves
1 large garlic clove, gently smashed and peeled
250–300g small lentils, rinsed and drained
450g radicchio, cut into 2.5cm-wide wedges, keeping the root end intact
fine sea salt and freshly ground black pepper
4 tablespoons good-quality extra virgin olive oil
a handful of flat-leaf parsley, finely chopped
2 teaspoons sherry vinegar

Cut the chorizo into 5mm cubes. In a medium saucepan, combine the chorizo and ½ tablespoon of oil. Cook over a medium heat for about 3 minutes, stirring occasionally, until the sausage begins to turn crispy. Use a rubber spatula to transfer the sausage and its oil to a plate.

Add 2 tablespoons of oil to the same saucepan with the onion, one-third of the chopped celery stalks, and the garlic. Cook over a low heat for a further 8 minutes, stirring occasionally, until the onion is softened.

Add the lentils and stir to combine. Add water to cover the lentils by about 3cm. Place over a high heat and bring to the boil, then reduce to a very gentle simmer and cook for 30–40 minutes until tender, stirring occasionally and adding water as necessary to keep the lentils covered.

Meanwhile, heat a griddle pan over a medium-high heat. Brush the radicchio with the remaining 2 tablespoons of oil and season generously with salt and pepper. Grill for about 8 minutes, turning regularly, until golden and tender. Transfer the radicchio to a chopping board, allow to cool for a few minutes, then coarsely chop and transfer to a large bowl.

When the lentils are tender, drain any liquid from the pan, then remove and discard the garlic. Spread the lentils on a baking tray set over a wire rack, leave to cool for 5–10 minutes, then add the lentils to the bowl with the radicchio. Add the remaining two-thirds of chopped celery stalks, celery leaves, good-quality oil, parsley, sherry vinegar and 1¼ teaspoons of salt. Toss to combine, then adust the seasoning, if necessary. Spoon the salad onto 4 plates, then spoon the chorizo and its oil over the top of each serving. Sprinkle with the celery leaves.

red quinoa, raw asparagus and chicory salad with shaved parmigiano-reggiano

I'm an ardent enthusiast of quinoa (pronounced keen-wah). Why? The slightly nutty light grain is rich in protein, antioxidants, easy-to-digest fibre and immune-system boosting amino acids. And it provides a delicious grain option for wheat- and gluten-free diets. I tend to opt for the heartier red and black varieties rather than white quinoa, but all three are terrific and any of them can be used here.

SERVES 4 TO 6

170g red quinoa, rinsed (see
  Box)
35g pine nuts
225g asparagus, trimmed
225g chicory
55g Parmigiano-Reggiano or
  Grana Padano cheese, very
  thinly shaved with a paring
  knife or vegetable peeler
4 tablespoons good-quality extra
  virgin olive oil
1 tablespoon fresh lemon juice
fine sea salt

Combine 480ml of water and the quinoa in a 1.4-litre saucepan and bring to the boil. Reduce the heat to a simmer, cover and cook for about 15 minutes until the water is absorbed.

Meanwhile, toast the pine nuts in a dry heavy-based frying pan over a medium-low heat for 4–6 minutes, stirring occasionally, until fragrant and a shade or two darker. Transfer the nuts to a plate to cool.

Spread the cooked quinoa on a baking tray set over a wire rack and leave to cool for 5–10 minutes. Meanwhile, cut the tips from the asparagus and quarter lengthways. Very thinly slice the stems crossways and on a slight diagonal. Cut the chicory crossways on a diagonal into 1cm-thick slices.

In a large serving bowl, combine the cooled quinoa, nuts, asparagus tips and stems, chicory, cheese, oil, lemon juice and ½ teaspoon of salt. Stir well before serving.

rinsing quinoa:

In its natural state, quinoa has a bitter-tasting saponin coating, which the plant produces to keep birds and insects at bay. Mostly this is removed commercially by polishing and pre-washing. If your quinoa has not been pre-washed, it is best to rinse it well before use to remove any saponin residue. Simply put the quinoa into a fine sieve and run cold water over it.

chickpea and morcilla sausage with wild rocket

Morcilla, a blood sausage flavoured with fresh onion and sweet spices, lends a rich meaty touch to this salad. Be sure to leave ample marinating time so that the chickpeas can take on the bright flavours of both the sausage and the tangy lemon dressing. Note: Morcilla is made with onions and sometimes rice. I use the non-rice version for this recipe as that is the type most readily available to me. If using the rice sort, it can be easier to crumble into the salad than to slice.

SERVES 4 TO 6

4 tablespoons fresh lemon juice
35g finely chopped shallot
fine sea salt
½ tablespoon extra virgin
  olive oil plus more for drizzling
150g morcilla sausage (see
  Sources, page 170)
3 stalks celery, cut into
  2.5cm matchsticks, plus
  3 tablespoons celery leaves
  (from the inner heart),
  coarsely chopped
2 x 410g tins chickpeas, rinsed
  and drained
2 tablespoons good-quality
  extra virgin olive oil, plus
  more for drizzling
¼ teaspoon paprika, preferably
  smoked (pimentón de la Vera)
  (see Sources, page 170), plus
  more for sprinkling
cayenne pepper
140g baby or wild rocket

Stir together the lemon juice, shallot and ½ teaspoon of salt in a small bowl, then set aside.

Heat the oil in a large non-stick frying pan over a medium-high heat. Add the sausage, reduce the heat to medium and cook for about 7 minutes, turning occasionally, until cooked through with a tender texture. Using tongs or a slotted spoon, transfer the sausage to a plate, reserving the pan with the oil and juices. Add the celery stalks to the pan, stir to coat with the oil and juices, and cook over a medium heat for 1 minute. Using a rubber spatula, scrape the celery and all of the pan juices into a large bowl.

Thinly slice the sausage and add it to the bowl with the celery. Add the reserved lemon juice mixture, chickpeas, good-quality oil, paprika, ½ teaspoon of salt and a pinch of cayenne pepper. Toss the salad to combine, cover and allow to marinate in the fridge for at least 3 hours or overnight.

About 1 hour before serving the salad, bring the chickpea and sausage mixture to room temperature. When ready to serve, gently toss with the wild rocket and celery leaves, and season with salt and cayenne pepper to taste. Serve the salad drizzled with a little good-quality oil and sprinkled with a pinch of paprika.

rice salad with tuna, roasted red peppers and pimento-stuffed olives

The bold flavours of this salad evoke a Spanish seaside meal. One of Steve's favourites, it's always a big hit at picnics and parties too. If you can't find jasmine rice, long-grain white rice will work here too.

SERVES 4 TO 6

2 large red peppers
1 large sweet white onion
2 tablespoons extra virgin olive oil
fine sea salt and freshly ground black pepper
225g Thai jasmine rice
3 tablespoons capers, preferably salt-packed
125g pimento-stuffed olives
340g tinned tuna in oil, drained
a handful of flat-leaf parsley, finely chopped, plus more for garnish
3 tablespoons good-quality extra virgin olive oil
2 tablespoons finely chopped chives, plus more for garnish
1 large lemon
flaky coarse sea salt

Preheat the oven to 200°C/gas mark 6. Line a baking tray with baking paper.

Cut the peppers into 1cm-wide strips. Cut the onion into 2cm-thick wedges, keeping the root end intact. Arrange both on the prepared baking tray in a single layer. Drizzle with the oil and season with ¼ teaspoon of fine sea salt and a generous pinch of pepper. Roast for 30–35 minutes, stirring once halfway through cooking, until the vegetables are tender and golden on the edges.

Meanwhile, rinse the rice well and drain. Add the rice to a large saucepan filled with 410ml of water, add ¼ teaspoon of fine sea salt and bring to the boil over a high heat. Reduce the heat to low, cover and cook for about 15 minutes until the rice is tender. Remove the pan from the heat and leave to stand, covered, for 15 minutes. Fluff the rice with a fork, then spread on a baking tray to cool.

Transfer the roasted vegetables on the baking paper to a wire rack to cool. Meanwhile, rinse the capers and soak in cold water for 10 minutes. Rinse again and coarsely chop. Drain and quarter the olives. Coarsely chop the cooled red peppers.

In a large bowl, combine the capers, olives, roasted vegetables, rice, 1 teaspoon of fine sea salt, tuna, parsley, 2 tablespoons of good-quality oil and the chives. Finely zest the lemon into the bowl. Stir well to combine. If time allows, chill the salad covered in the fridge for 3 hours or overnight.

Transfer the salad to a serving bowl and allow it to come to room temperature, if it has been chilled. Drizzle with the remaining 1 tablespoon of good-quality oil, then sprinkle with a generous pinch or two of flaky coarse sea salt. Garnish with parsley and chives.

barley and roasted aubergine salad

Those who like baba ghanoush will enjoy the smoky quality of the roasted aubergine in this warm salad. Try pairing it with grilled sausages or fish.

SERVES 4

680g aubergine
4 tablespoons extra virgin
   olive oil
fine sea salt and freshly ground
   black pepper
140g pearl barley
a small bunch of flat-leaf parsley,
   coarsely chopped, plus more
   for garnish
3 tablespoons finely chopped
   mint, plus more for garnish
1 small garlic clove, coarsely
   chopped
1½ teaspoons deseeded and
   finely chopped serrano chilli
½ teaspoon dried oregano
1 large lemon
115g feta cheese, crumbled

Place a rack in the middle of the oven and preheat to 200°C/gas mark 6. Line a baking tray with baking paper.

Halve the aubergine lengthways and score the flesh in a criss-cross pattern. Brush the flesh sides with 1 tablespoon of the oil and season with a generous pinch of salt and pepper. Arrange the aubergine halves, cut sides down, on the prepared baking tray and roast for 45–50 minutes, until the flesh is tender.

Meanwhile, bring a large pan of salted water to the boil and cook the barley for about 45 minutes, until tender yet still firm to the bite. Drain, then spread the barley on a baking tray set over a wire rack to cool.

Transfer the baking tray with the roasted aubergine to another wire rack. Turn the aubergine halves cut sides up and leave to cool for 5 minutes, then scrape the flesh from the skins, transfer to a fine-mesh sieve set over a bowl and leave to drain for 30 minutes.

Mound the parsley, mint, garlic, chilli and oregano on a chopping board and finely chop together.

In a large frying pan, heat the remaining 3 tablespoons of oil over a medium-high heat. Add the herb and spice mixture, reduce the heat to low and cook, stirring frequently, for 3 minutes. Stir in the aubergine and cook for a further minute. Remove the pan from the heat.

Transfer the aubergine mixture to a large bowl. Add the barley and toss together to combine. Finely zest the lemon into the bowl, then squeeze enough lemon to make 1½ tablespoons of juice and add to the bowl. Add half of the cheese, ¼ teaspoon of salt and toss together to combine. Serve the salad warm or at room temperature, garnished with the remaining cheese and more fresh herbs.

chapter five:

frisée and fried oysters with buttermilk-chive dressing

My friend Cameron showed me this simple way to shallow-fry oysters, without the fuss of dipping in egg and dusting with flour. The technique makes for a clean, full-tilt oyster flavour that nicely complements the slight bitterness of the greens, wisps of thinly shaved fennel and creamy chive dressing. Any oyster variety works well here: tiny, sweet and lemony or plump and briny... Choose whichever are the freshest and the kind that you like.

SERVES 4

DRESSING
240ml buttermilk
120ml Greek yogurt (see Box, page 84)
5 tablespoons finely chopped chives
4 tablespoons mayonnaise
1 lemon
fine sea salt and freshly ground black pepper

115g fine cornmeal
½ teaspoon dried thyme
⅛ teaspoon cayenne pepper
fine sea salt and freshly ground black pepper
225g frisée, torn
1 small fennel bulb, very thinly shaved
24 oysters, shucked and drained
about 8 tablespoons extra virgin olive oil for frying
flaky coarse sea salt

To make the dressing, combine the buttermilk, yogurt, chives and mayonnaise in a medium bowl. Grate the zest from the lemon into the bowl, then squeeze enough lemon to make about 20ml of juice. Add the juice, a scant ½ teaspoon of fine sea salt and a generous pinch of black pepper, and whisk to combine well.

Place the cornmeal in a second medium bowl. Sprinkle with the thyme, then add the cayenne pepper, ¼ teaspoon of fine sea salt and a generous pinch of black pepper. Mix to combine using a dry whisk.

Place the frisée, fennel and a generous pinch of black pepper in a large bowl and toss together to mix.

Line a large plate with kitchen paper. Drop the oysters into the cornmeal mixture a few at a time and toss to coat well.

Pour enough oil into a large frying pan to come about 5mm of the way up the sides of the pan. Heat over a medium heat until the oil is shimmering and fragrant. Fry the oysters in 2 batches for about 10 minutes, turning once, until lightly golden and crisp on both sides. Using a slotted spoon, transfer the oysters to the prepared plate to drain.

Mound nice high piles of the frisée mixture onto 4 serving plates. Arrange the fried oysters tucked between the leaves and on the plate. Drizzle the dressing over the salads, then sprinkle with pinches of flaky coarse sea salt. Serve immediately.

crab-stuffed grilled squid with shaved courgette and sweetcorn salad

Thinly shaved raw courgettes have a sweet flavour and delicate texture. They are delicious combined with other ingredients or on their own with a drizzle of good olive oil and a generous sprinkling of flaky sea salt. Squid tip: If you're using the barbecue rather than a griddle pan to cook the squid, skewer the tentacles to prevent them from falling through the grate.

SERVES 4

225g fresh white crab meat, picked over

2 tablespoons mayonnaise

fine sea salt and freshly ground black pepper

8 cleaned squid bodies (8–12cm each) plus 16 tentacles

3½ tablespoons extra virgin olive oil, plus more for grilling

1 corn on the cob, kernels removed (see Box)

1 tablespoon finely chopped shallot

170g cherry or grape tomatoes, halved or quartered, if large

340g courgettes or summer squash, or a mix, trimmed

a handful of basil leaves, large ones torn

Mix together the crab, mayonnaise, ⅛ teaspoon of salt and a generous pinch of pepper. Using your fingers, gently but firmly stuff the squid bodies with pinches of the crab mixture, leaving a 1cm space at the top. Seal the squid tops using toothpicks.

Heat 1 tablespoon of the oil in a medium frying pan over a medium-high heat. Add the sweetcorn, shallot, ⅛ teaspoon of salt and a generous pinch of pepper. Reduce the heat to medium-low and cook for about 3 minutes, stirring occasionally, until tender. Add the tomatoes, toss and cook for 1 minute. Transfer to a plate and leave to cool.

Using a vegetable peeler, and working lengthways, slice the courgettes and/or summer squash into ribbons. Place in a bowl, add 2 tablespoons of the oil, the basil and a few generous pinches of salt and pepper, and gently toss together.

Heat the barbecue to medium-high or heat a griddle pan over a medium-high heat. Drizzle the squid with the remaining ½ tablespoon of oil and season with salt and pepper. Lightly brush the barbecue rack or griddle pan with oil, then grill the squid bodies and tentacles, turning frequently, until golden in spots and cooked through, 2–3 minutes for the tentacles and 13–15 minutes for the bodies. As the squid pieces are cooked, transfer them to a large plate.

Divide the courgette salad and the squid bodies and tentacles among 4 serving plates, then arrange the sweetcorn mixture on top.

how to safely cut kernels from a corn on the cob:

Lightly dampen a tea towel and lay it flat under your chopping board to prevent it from slipping. Remove the husk and any silky threads from a corn on the cob then, using a sharp knife, cut the cob in half crossways. Stand one half of the cob flat end down on the board, then cut the kernels from the cob in sections, keeping the knife blade close to the core and slicing in a downwards motion.

roasted cod salad with turkish tarator and caramelised shallots and orange slices

In many Middle Eastern countries, tarator is a sesame dip, but in Turkey it is a yogurt sauce flavoured with walnuts, garlic and bread. Roasted orange slices provide a sweet and tangy citrus counterpoint to the richness of the sauce and fish. To make nicely roasted pieces, the trick is to use a good sharp knife to create uniform slices and keep a close watch while they roast, moving slices from the outer edges of the tray into the middle as they brown. I love the sweet juiciness of Valencia oranges, which are available from February to October, with peak season in May, June and July. If you can't find Valencia oranges, use any juicy sweet orange you like.

SERVES 4

1 x 600g skinless cod fillet,
   about 2cm thick
fine sea salt and freshly
   ground black pepper
5½ tablespoons extra
   virgin olive oil
1 Valencia orange, ends
   trimmed, cut crossways
   into 3mm-thick slices
340g shallots, peeled,
   separated at the root if there
   is more than 1 bulb in
   the skin, and cut in half
   or quartered
115g mixed greens
1½ teaspoons fresh lemon juice
good-quality extra virgin
   olive oil
flaky coarse sea salt

TARATOR

1 piece of baguette, about
   10cm long
2 garlic cloves, coarsely
   chopped
fine sea salt
100g walnut pieces
1 lemon
4 tablespoons extra virgin
   olive oil
5 tablespoons Greek yogurt
   (see Box, page 84)
2 tablespoons water

Place racks in the middle and lower third of the oven and preheat to 190°C/gas mark 5.

Make the tarator. Remove and discard the crust from the baguette, then cut the bread into 1cm cubes (you should have about 25g). Soak the bread cubes in cold water for 1 minute, then gently but firmly squeeze out and discard the liquid. Using the blade and flat side of a chef's knife, coarsely chop and mash together the garlic and salt into a paste. Set the paste and bread aside.

Place the walnuts in the bowl of a food processor and pulse until finely chopped. Finely zest the lemon into the bowl. Squeeze enough lemon to make 2 tablespoons of juice then add to the bowl along with the bread and garlic paste and purée to make a thick paste. With the machine running, add the oil in a slow and steady stream, stopping and scraping down the sides of the bowl, until all the oil is incorporated. Add the yogurt and water, and purée. Transfer to a sealed container and refrigerate for up to 2 days.

Season the cod on both sides with fine sea salt and pepper, then place in a baking dish and drizzle with 1 tablespoon of oil. Line a baking tray with baking paper. Arrange the orange slices in a single layer on top. Drizzle with 1 tablespoon of oil and season generously with fine sea salt and pepper. In a bowl, toss the shallots with 2 tablespoons of oil, ¼ teaspoon of fine sea salt and several generous grinds of pepper. Arrange the shallots in a single layer in a baking dish.

Place the oranges on the middle rack of the oven and the cod and shallots on the lower rack. Roast, turning all the trays and stirring the shallots after 10 minutes. After another 8–10 minutes, the cod will be opaque and just cooked through. Transfer to a wire rack and leave to cool to room temperature. Keep a close eye on the oranges, waiting until the edges are mid-dark golden, about another 5 minutes. If the shallots are tender and golden, remove them from the oven, or continue roasting for another 5 minutes. Transfer the orange slices to a chopping board. Cut large slices in half or quarters and leave small slices whole.

In a bowl, toss together the frisée, remaining 1½ tablespoons of oil, the lemon juice and a generous pinch each of fine sea salt and pepper. Taste and adjust the seasoning. Spread the tarator on the serving plates and mound the greens on top. Using a spatula, divide the fish into 4 pieces (it's OK if the pieces break apart) and place on top of the greens. Top with the orange pieces and shallots. Drizzle with the good-quality oil and sprinkle with flaky coarse sea salt and pepper. The remaining tarator can be served at the table or saved for use as a dip.

pan-fried squid in a mound of greens with seared aubergine and blistered tomatoes

I like to include a peppery variety in the mix of greens here – a mix of rocket, mizuna leaves, baby mustard greens or watercress – to complement the sweetness of the aubergine and the tang of the tomatoes. Choose whatever is freshest at your local farmers' market or supermarket.

SERVES 4

600g cleaned squid bodies
  and tentacles
fine sea salt and freshly ground
  black pepper
1 garlic clove, gently smashed
  and peeled
8 tablespoons extra virgin
  olive oil
340g aubergine, cut into
  5mm cubes
170g cherry or grape tomatoes
45g black olives in brine, stoned
  and coarsely chopped
1½ tablespoons fresh
  lemon juice
½ teaspoon Sriracha (see
  Sources, page 170) or
  other hot chilli sauce
170g mixed greens
2 tablespoons finely chopped
  fresh mint

Place the squid bodies and tentacles and a generous pinch each of salt and pepper in a large frying pan. Add water to come three-quarters of the way up the sides of the squid. Bring to a simmer over a medium-high heat, then reduce to a gentle simmer and cook for about 20 minutes, stirring occasionally, until the squid is tender. Add water if necessary to keep the liquid halfway up the sides of the squid.

Using a slotted spoon, transfer the squid to a bowl. Add the garlic to the pan juices and cook over a high heat for 7–9 minutes, until reduced to 2–3 tablespoons. Meanwhile, cut the squid bodies crossways into 3cm-wide rings. If the tentacles are large, slice them in half. Pat dry with kitchen paper. Transfer the juices to a small bowl, discarding the garlic, and set aside.

Heat 2 tablespoons of the oil in a large non-stick frying pan over a high heat until hot but not smoking. Add half of the aubergine, season with a generous pinch each of salt and pepper and cook in a single layer for 3–4 minutes, turning the pieces occasionally, until tender and browned. Transfer to a large mixing bowl. Repeat the process, heating 1 tablespoon of oil in the pan and using the remaining aubergine and an additional generous pinch each of salt and pepper.

Using the same pan, add 1 tablespoon of oil and heat over a high heat. Add the tomatoes, season with a generous pinch each of salt and pepper and cook for about 2 minutes, occasionally gently moving the pan over the heat to roll the tomatoes, until blistered and collapsed. Add the olives and stir to combine, then, using a slotted spoon, transfer to the mixing bowl and leave to cool. Add 1 tablespoon of oil to the pan and heat over medium-high. Add the squid pieces and cook for about 5 minutes until crisped, stirring occasionally and using a screen if the oil is splattering. Remove from the heat and season the squid with ¼ teaspoon of salt and a generous pinch of pepper.

In a large mixing bowl, whisk together the remaining 3 tablespoons of oil, lemon juice, Sriracha, ⅛ teaspoon of salt and a generous pinch of pepper. Add the greens and toss to combine, then add the squid and squid juices, and toss again. Adjust the seasoning to taste. Divide the salad among 4 serving plates. Gently stir the mint into the aubergine mixture, then arrange on top of and around the salads.

grilled prawn salad with a minted pea purée and tender greens

This quick and simple salad evokes springtime but can be made any time of the year as it employs one of my favourite kitchen staples: frozen peas.

SERVES 4

16 large prawns, peeled and
    deveined
2 tablespoons extra virgin
    olive oil
1½ teaspoons finely chopped
    garlic
⅛ teaspoon cayenne pepper
2 teaspoons fresh lemon juice
1 teaspoon finely chopped shallot
fine sea salt and freshly ground
    black pepper
340g red-leaf or butterhead
    lettuce
2 tablespoons good-quality
    extra virgin olive oil
flaky coarse sea salt
1½ tablespoons finely chopped
    chives, plus chive flowers if
    available

PEA PURÉE
190g frozen peas
a handful of mint leaves
3½ tablespoons extra virgin
    olive oil
¾ teaspoon fresh lemon zest
fine sea salt and freshly ground
    black pepper

Put the prawns, oil, garlic and cayenne pepper in a bowl, toss together, then set aside.

In a large bowl, whisk together the lemon juice, shallot, ¼ teaspoon of fine sea salt and ⅛ teaspoon of black pepper. Leave to stand for 10 minutes.

Meanwhile, make the pea purée. Cook the peas in a saucepan of boiling salted water for 3 minutes, then drain under cold running water to cool. In a blender, combine the peas, 2 tablespoons of cold water, the mint, oil, lemon zest, a scant ½ teaspoon of salt and ⅛ teaspoon of pepper. Purée until smooth.

Heat the barbecue to medium-high or place a griddle pan over a medium-high heat. (If using the barbecue, thread the prawns onto skewers.) Grill the prawns for 4–5 minutes, turning once or twice, until opaque and just cooked through, then transfer to a large plate.

Trim the lettuce head and separate the leaves, tearing large leaves into pieces. Add the good-quality oil to the shallot mixture and whisk to combine. Add the lettuce and gently toss to combine well. Season with flaky coarse sea salt and black pepper to taste.

Place a dollop of pea purée into the centre of 4 serving plates and spread to about 3mm thick. Mound the greens on top, then sprinkle with the chives and chive flowers, if using. Arrange the prawns on the plates and sprinkle with flaky coarse sea salt.

lobster salad with lemon-basil mayonnaise and fresh tomatoes

This salad is a celebration of summer and over-the-top delicious. Bookended by fresh corn on the cob, drizzled with olive oil and sprinkled with sea salt and coarsely crushed pepper, and a warm plum cobbler topped with cinnamon ice cream, it's also the centrepiece of one of my favourite seasonal meals. Be sure to use tomatoes at their juicy sweet peak. The lobsters can be cooked, shelled and, if you like, prepared as a salad one day ahead then covered and chilled.

SERVES 4 TO 6

2 lemons
5 tablespoons finely chopped
   red onion
fine sea salt
4 x 680g live lobsters
80ml mayonnaise
2 tablespoons thinly sliced basil
   leaves, plus a handful of leaves,
   large ones torn
freshly ground black pepper
680g cherry and/or small
   heirloom tomatoes, cores
   removed, cut into 1cm pieces
1½ tablespoons good-quality
   extra virgin olive oil, plus
   more for drizzling
flaky coarse sea salt

Bring a large 8-litre stockpot of salted water to the boil.

Meanwhile, finely grate the zest of the lemons into a large bowl. Squeeze the lemons to make 4 tablespoons of juice and add it to the bowl. Add the onion and ½ teaspoon of fine sea salt and stir together. Leave to stand at room temperature.

Plunge 2 lobsters head first into the boiling water. Loosely cover the pot and cook the lobsters for 9 minutes from the time they enter the water, then, using tongs, transfer to the sink to cool. Return the water to the boil and cook the remaining 2 lobsters in the same way.

When the lobsters are cool, remove the meat from the claws, knuckles and tails. Discard the tomalley (the soft green paste found in the body cavity) and any roe and shells (or save for another use). Cut the meat into 1cm pieces.

Add the mayonnaise, sliced basil leaves and ¼ teaspoon of black pepper to the onion mixture and whisk together to combine. Add the lobster meat and gently stir the salad together. In a large bowl, gently toss the tomatoes, torn basil leaves, oil, pinches of flaky coarse sea salt and black pepper to taste.

Mound the tomato salad in the centre of 4 serving plates. Top with the lobster salad, then drizzle with any leftover juices from both bowls. Drizzle with oil and sprinkle with an extra pinch of flaky coarse sea salt.

best kitchen scissors:

For as long as I can remember, I've had the same pair of red-handled, razor-sharp Joyce Chen kitchen scissors, which are excellent for countless food-prep chores, including snipping through tough lobster bodies and knuckles to remove whole chunks of meat. It's always helpful to have a pair of quality, ultra-sharp scissors to hand.

grilled baby octopus with crispy potatoes and smoked paprika aïoli

Popular Mediterranean cuisine, baby octopus may seem intimidating, but in fact is simple to prepare. The aromatics that season the cooking stock can be varied (a great way to use up valuable scraps): fennel stalks, a lone carrot and/or a gently smashed garlic clove can be used in addition to or in place of the onion and celery. Be sure to allow time to marinate the octopus; it's best if done overnight, but a few hours will suffice. If using a barbecue (as opposed to a griddle pan), thread the octopus onto skewers to prevent the pieces from falling through the grate. The aioli here is purposely loose, which makes it easy to drizzle.

OCTOPUS

300ml dry white wine

1 small onion, peeled and
quartered

1 celery stalk, cut into 3 pieces

5 leafy sprigs flat-leaf parsley,
plus 3 tablespoons finely
chopped flat-leaf parsley,
plus extra leaves for garnish

3 lemons

900g cleaned baby octopus

1 Valencia or juice orange

4 tablespoons extra virgin
olive oil

4 tablespoons dry white wine

3 garlic cloves, thinly sliced

¼ teaspoon smoked paprika

freshly ground black pepper
and fine sea salt

POTATOES

790g fingerling or other
small potatoes

4 tablespoons extra virgin
olive oil

¾ teaspoon smoked paprika

fine sea salt and freshly ground
black pepper

a small handful of flat-leaf
parsley leaves

SMOKED PAPRIKA AIOLI

1 large garlic clove, coarsely
chopped

fine sea salt

1 Valencia or other sweet orange

6 tablespoons mayonnaise

¼ teaspoon plus ⅛ teaspoon
smoked paprika

To prepare the octopus, put 1.4 litres of water, 300ml wine, onion, celery and parsley sprigs in a large, heavy-based pan. Cut 1 lemon in half and, over a fine-mesh sieve, squeeze the juice into the liquid mixture. Discard the seeds, then add the lemon halves to the pan. Bring the liquid to a gentle simmer, add the octopus and cook for about 20 minutes, stirring occasionally, until tender.

Meanwhile, finely grate the zest of 1 lemon and the orange into a large bowl. Quarter the fruit and, over a fine-mesh sieve, squeeze the juice into the bowl, then discard the seeds and add the rinds. Add the oil, 4 tablespoons of wine, chopped parsley, garlic, paprika and ¼ teaspoon of pepper.

Drain the cooked octopus and discard the aromatics. Cut the octopus in halves or quarters, depending on size, then add to the bowl with the marinade. Cover and marinate, stirring occasionally, for 3 hours or overnight.

To prepare the potatoes, place them in a large pan and cover with water by about 5cm. Bring to the boil and cook for 10–15 minutes until tender. Drain, then place the potatoes on a wire rack to cool completely.

Meanwhile, make the aioli. Using the blade and flat side of a chef's knife, coarsely chop and mash together the garlic and salt into a paste. Transfer the paste into a medium bowl. Finely grate the orange zest over the bowl, then squeeze the orange to make 3 tablespoons of juice and add it to the bowl. Add the mayonnaise and paprika, and whisk to combine. Refrigerate, covered, until ready to use.

Cut the cooled potatoes crossways into 5mm rounds and place in a large bowl. Add 2 tablespoons of the oil, the paprika, ½ teaspoon of salt and ¼ teaspoon of pepper. Toss to combine.

In a 30cm non-stick frying pan, heat 1 tablespoon of the remaining oil over a high heat until hot but not smoking. Add half of the potatoes and spread to the edges of the pan. Cook for about 6 minutes until crispy on the undersides, then turn over and cook until golden on the undersides, about 3 minutes more. Transfer to a large bowl and repeat with the remaining tablespoon of oil and potatoes. While the potatoes are hot, add ½ teaspoon of salt, a generous pinch of pepper and the parsley to the bowl. Toss to combine.

Remove the octopus from the marinade and season with salt and pepper. Heat a griddle pan over a medium-high heat. Grill the octopus for 10–12 minutes, turning occasionally, until golden and crispy on the edges.

Divide the potatoes among 4 serving plates. Top with the octopus, drizzle with the aioli and garnish with a few parsley leaves.

warm prawn salad with indian-spiced lentils, yogurt and pumpkin seeds

SERVES 4

½ teaspoon fennel seeds
1 lemon
16 large prawns, peeled and
  deveined
1½ tablespoons finely chopped
  peeled ginger
4 tablespoons extra virgin
  olive oil
cayenne pepper
175g small green or brown
  lentils, sorted to remove
  debris and rinsed
1 large garlic clove, gently
  smashed and peeled,
  plus 1 large garlic clove,
  finely chopped
fine sea salt
½ teaspoon plus ⅛ teaspoon
  turmeric
¼ teaspoon ground cumin

SPINACH
1 tablespoon finely
  chopped shallot
2 teaspoons fresh lemon juice
fine sea salt
3 tablespoons Greek yogurt
3 tablespoons extra virgin
  olive oil
freshly ground black pepper
cayenne pepper
225g baby spinach
1½ tablespoons coarsely
  chopped coriander
4 teaspoons roasted shelled
  pumpkin seeds (pepitas)

Pepitas (roasted shelled pumpkin seeds) add pop and texture to this earthy warm salad. The seeds lend additional protein as well as iron and other nutrients too. Look for them at health food shops and large supermarkets.

In a small frying pan, toast the fennel seeds over a medium-low heat for about 3 minutes, shaking the pan back and forth over the heat until fragrant and lightly toasted. Transfer to a spice grinder or pestle and mortar and finely grind. Finely zest the lemon into a medium bowl, then add the ground fennel, prawns, ½ tablespoon ginger, 2 tablespoons of oil and ⅛ teaspoon of cayenne pepper. Toss to combine well and set aside.

Place the lentils, the gently smashed garlic clove, a scant ½ teaspoon of salt and ½ teaspoon of turmeric in a medium saucepan. Add water to cover by 5cm. Bring the mixture just to the boil, then reduce to a gentle simmer and cook for 25–30 minutes until tender, stirring occasionally and adding water if necessary to keep the lentils covered.

Drain the lentils and place in a bowl. In a medium non-stick frying pan, heat the remaining 2 tablespoons of oil over a medium-high heat until hot but not smoking. Remove the pan from the heat, then stir in the chopped garlic, remaining tablespoon ginger, cumin, remaining ⅛ teaspoon of turmeric and a pinch of cayenne pepper. Leave to stand for 1 minute, then add the mixture to the lentils and stir to combine. Cover to keep warm.

Return the frying pan to a medium-high heat. Add the prawns with any oil and spices from the bowl and ⅛ teaspoon of salt. Cook for 2–3 minutes, stirring occasionally, until the prawns are opaque and just cooked through. Transfer to a bowl.

To make the salad, stir together the shallot, lemon juice and salt in a large bowl, then leave to stand for 10 minutes. Add the yogurt, oil and a pinch each of black and cayenne pepper, and whisk to combine well. Add the spinach and gently toss to combine.

Arrange the spinach on 4 serving plates. Top with the warm lentils and prawns. Sprinkle the salads with the coriander and pumpkin seeds.

frisée salad with seared scallops and salsa verde

SERVES 4

SALSA VERDE
1½ tablespoons capers,
  preferably salt-packed
  (see Box, page 32)
6 tablespoons finely chopped
  flat-leaf parsley
3 tablespoons finely chopped
  chives
2 teaspoons finely chopped
  shallot
1 oil-packed anchovy fillet, finely
  chopped
1 lemon
6 tablespoons extra virgin olive
  oil

340g frisée, torn
12 diver-caught scallops
  (1–1¼ pounds), washed and
  patted dry
fine sea salt
1 tablespoon extra virgin
  olive oil for frying
30g coarsely chopped roasted
  unsalted almonds
coarsely cracked black pepper

Here's a perfect example of how a favourite sauce – Italian salsa verde – can be a stupendous salad dressing. Capers and anchovies, which I consider the great character actors of the kitchen, are subtle yet key flavour ingredients here and should not be skipped or skimped on. For best flavour, purchase salt-packed capers rather than those preserved in brine when you can.

First make the salsa verde. Rinse the capers and soak them in cold water for 10 minutes. Rinse again and finely chop. Place in a bowl with the parsley, chives, shallot and anchovy. Finely grate the zest of the lemon into the bowl, holding the lemon close to the bowl to capture the flavourful oil. Squeeze the lemon to make 3 tablespoons of juice and add to the salsa verde with the oil. Stir to combine.

Place the frisée in a large bowl and set aside.

Lightly season the scallops with salt. Heat the oil in a large non-stick frying pan over a medium-high heat until hot but not smoking. Add the scallops and cook for 1½–2 minutes on each side, until brown and just opaque in the centre. Remove the pan from the heat.

Sprinkle the frisée with ¼ teaspoon of salt, then add the salsa verde and toss to combine well. Divide the greens and scallops among 4 serving plates, then sprinkle with the almonds and cracked black pepper.

manila clams with asparagus, baby spinach and jamón

I like to serve this Spanish-style salad as a light lunch tapas (it's lovely paired with the octopus salad on page 128, the chickpea and morcilla salad on page 112, and a salad or two from chapter one) or as a starter to a larger meal of Spanish dishes, perhaps fabada Asturiana (a rich bean stew) or a pot of Moorish braised oxtail. Whether you serve the salad on its own or with other dishes, a crisp, dry version of the lightly effervescent Basque wine Txakoli makes a nice accompaniment.

SERVES 4

1 lime
2 tablespoons finely chopped
  shallot
fine sea salt and freshly ground
  black pepper
6 tablespoons extra virgin
  olive oil
680g Manila or other small
  clams, scrubbed clean
30g (3mm-thick sliced) jamón
  serrano or prosciutto, cut
  into matchsticks
1 serrano chilli, thinly sliced
  crossways with seeds
225g asparagus, trimmed
  and cut crosswise into
  2.5cm lengths
1 large garlic clove, very
  thinly sliced
1 tablespoon finely chopped
  flat-leaf parsley
225g baby spinach

Zest the lime into a medium bowl. Squeeze the lime to make 1½ tablespoons of juice then add the juice to the bowl. Add the shallot, ¼ teaspoon of salt and a generous pinch of pepper. Stir to combine and set aside.

In a 30cm frying pan, heat 2 tablespoons of the oil over a medium-high heat until hot but not smoking. Add the clams, jamón and chilli, and cook for about 5 minutes until the clams are opened, occasionally lifting the pan slightly off the heat and shaking it back and forth. Add the asparagus, garlic and parsley. Using a wooden spoon, gently stir so that the newly added ingredients get tucked into the pan juices. Cook for a further 2 minutes.

Remove the pan from the heat. Using a slotted spoon, transfer the clams to a bowl and discard any unopened clams. Transfer the asparagus mixture to a second bowl. Drain the pan juices through a muslin-lined sieve into a third bowl.

Add 2 teaspoons of the pan juices to the reserved shallot mixture, then add the remaining oil in a slow and steady stream, whisking continuously, until the dressing is emulsified.

Divide the spinach, clams and asparagus mixture among 4 serving plates. Drizzle with the dressing and serve immediately.

sardines with lamb's lettuce, shaved fennel and grilled lemon

This simple salad defies seasons – it makes a fitting lunch on a hot summer's afternoon, a nice starter for a winter festive meal or a nutrient-packed anytime dish. Serve it family-style from a large platter or as individual servings on pretty plates. If cooking on a barbecue, use a grill tray to prevent the lemon slices from slipping into the coals. If you can't find mache, any small tender lettuce will do.

SERVES 4

1 medium fennel bulb, including
  stems and fronds
8 fresh sardines, cleaned,
  leaving head and tail intact
2 lemons
3 tablespoons extra virgin
  olive oil, plus more for
  brushing
½ teaspoon Aleppo pepper or
  pinch cayenne
fine sea salt and freshly ground
  black pepper
115g lamb's lettuce

Finely chop half the fennel, including half the fronds.

Rinse the sardines and pat dry, then spread out on a platter. Finely zest 1 lemon over the top, turning the sardines halfway through, to cover both sides. Drizzle the sardines with ½ tablespoon of the oil and sprinkle the outside and cavities with the fennel stems, the Aleppo pepper and a generous ¼ teaspoon of salt.

Squeeze 2 teaspoons of juice from the zested lemon into a small bowl and set aside. Cut the remaining whole lemon crossways into 3mm-thick rounds. Remove and discard the seeds.

Heat a barbecue or a griddle pan until hot. Brush with oil and grill the sardines, in 2 batches if necessary, for 4–5 minutes per batch, turning once until just cooked through. Using a metal spatula, transfer the cooked fish to a clean large plate.

Lightly season the lemon slices with salt and black pepper, then grill for about 1 minute on each side until lightly charred. Transfer to a large bowl.

Thinly shave the remaining half fennel bulb and place in the bowl with the lemon. Add the reserved lemon juice, the remaining 2½ tablespoons of oil, half the fennel fronds, ½ teaspoon salt and a generous pinch of black pepper; toss to combine. Add the lamb's lettuce and very gently toss to combine.

Divide the salad and the sardines among 4 serving plates and garnish with the remaining fennel fronds.

warm tuna brochettes over a mediterranean tomato salad

On a warm summer's afternoon or evening, heaven to me is this simple salad of tuna skewers spiced with toasted fennel and cumin seeds, served over a mix of fresh tomatoes and olives. When available, a mix of colourful heirloom tomatoes, small and large varieties, is nice. Soaking thinly sliced onion in a few changes of ice water removes the bite.

SERVES 4

70g very thinly sliced red onion
¾ teaspoon fennel seeds
¾ teaspoon cumin seeds
1 lemon
fine sea salt and freshly ground black pepper
⅛ teaspoon cayenne pepper
450g fresh tuna steaks, cut into 2.5cm cubes
680g tomatoes
100g mixed olives, stoned and coarsely chopped
10g coriander leaves
3 tablespoons good-quality extra virgin olive oil
1 tablespoon plus 1 teaspoon red wine vinegar
flaky coarse sea salt

metal or wooden skewers

Submerge the onion in a small bowl of ice cold water and leave to stand for 10 minutes, then drain. Repeat twice more. If using wooden skewers, soak in water for 10 minutes

Meanwhile, toast the fennel and cumin seeds together in a small frying pan over a medium-low heat for about 3 minutes, shaking the pan back and forth, until fragrant and lightly toasted. Transfer to a spice grinder and grind or finely chop together.

Finely zest the lemon into a medium bowl. Add the ground spices, ¼ teaspoon of fine sea salt, ⅛ teaspoon of black pepper and the cayenne pepper. Stir to combine well, then add the tuna cubes and toss to coat. Thread the cubes onto skewers.

Heat a barbecue to medium-high or heat a griddle pan over a medium-high heat. Grill the tuna for 2–3 minutes until browned on all sides but still pink in the middle, then transfer to a large plate.

Pat dry the soaked onion. Cut the tomatoes into small pieces. In a large bowl, combine the onion, tomatoes, olives, coriander, oil, vinegar and ⅛ teaspoon of black pepper. Sprinkle with ½ teaspoon of flaky coarse sea salt, toss to combine, then adjust the seasoning to taste.

Mound the tomato salad onto 4 serving plates and top with the tuna brochettes.

peppery red snapper salad with crispy *tostones*

This lively salad is substantial enough for a meal. *Tostones* – crisp, pan-fried plantains – are easy to make and especially delicious with this vinegary, garlicky Caribbean salad.

SERVES 4

2 x 790g whole red snappers (sustainably sourced), cleaned and leaving head and tail intact
fine sea salt and freshly ground black pepper
2 tablespoons fresh lime juice
1 tablespoon extra virgin olive oil, plus more for greasing

SAUCE
135ml cider vinegar
3 spring onions, whites and greens, very thinly sliced
3 serrano chillies, seeded and finely chopped
3 large garlic cloves, finely chopped
3 tablespoons grapeseed oil
scant ½ teaspoon fine sea salt

DRESSING
2 limes
2 tablespoons finely chopped shallot
fine sea salt
3 tablespoons grapeseed oil
1 tablespoon honey

TOSTONES
3 green plantains
vegetable oil for frying
fine sea salt

680g Chinese cabbage, very thinly sliced
2 tablespoons coarsely chopped coriander

Place a rack in the middle of the oven and preheat to 200°C/gas mark 6. Lay each fish on its side. With a paring knife, cut three 6cm-long vertical slits through the skin and partially into the flesh. Repeat on the other side. Pat dry.

Grease a heavy-based 33 x 23cm roasting tin. Lay the fish in the tin in a single layer, head to tail. Season all over with 1 teaspoon salt and ½ teaspoon pepper, then drizzle with the lime juice and oil. Roast uncovered for about 30 minutes, rotating the tin and flipping the fish once halfway through, until opaque and just cooked through. Meanwhile, prepare the sauce and dressing.

For the sauce, whisk together all of the ingredients in a medium bowl. For the dressing, finely zest 1 lime into a large bowl, then squeeze the 2 limes to make 3 tablespoons of juice. Add the lime juice, shallot and ½ teaspoon of salt to the bowl. Leave to stand for 10 minutes, then whisk in the oil and honey.

When the fish is done, transfer the pan to a wire rack. When the fish is cool enough to handle, run a paring knife down the spine of each fish. Use a spatula to lift the top fillet off the bones and transfer to a plate. Starting with the tail end, lift off and discard the backbone and head. Remove any bones from the top and bottom fillets. Use your hands to gently break the fillets into small pieces.

To make the tostones, line a large plate with kitchen paper. Peel and cut the plaintains crossways into 2.5cm pieces. Add enough oil to a large frying pan to come 5mm up the sides. Heat the oil over a medium heat until hot but not smoking. Fry the plantain pieces, cut sides down, for about 5 minutes, turning once until golden. Transfer to kitchen paper to drain and reserve the pan.

While still warm, place one plaintain at a time, cut side up, between 2 pieces of kitchen paper. Pressing with your palm, flatten to about 5mm thick.

Return the frying pan to a medium heat. When the oil is hot, fry the tostones in batches for about 1 minute, turning once, until lightly golden on both sides. Transfer to fresh kitchen paper to drain. While hot, sprinkle the tostones generously with salt.

Add the cabbage to the dressing and toss to combine. Divide the salad and fish among 4 serving plates. Sprinkle with the coriander. Arrange the hot tostones on the plates. Spoon 3 tablespoons of the sauce over the top of each plate and use the rest for dipping the tostones. Serve immediately.

smoked trout salad with pickled beets, cucumber and roasted almonds

SERVES 4

HERB-ALMOND CREAM
8 tablespoons sour cream
5 tablespoons finely chopped
** mixed fresh herbs**
6 tablespoons finely chopped
** roasted unsalted almonds**
fine sea salt

3 tablespoons extra virgin
** olive oil**
1½ tablespoons fresh
** lemon juice**
fine sea salt and freshly ground
** black pepper**
2 pickling or 3 Persian (mini,
** seedless) cucumbers**
115g baby rocket
about 10 radishes, very
** thinly sliced**
70g pickled beetroot, cut into
** matchsticks**
115g smoked trout, skin and any
** small bones removed, broken**
** into bite-sized pieces**

A packet of smoked trout is a great item to keep in the fridge. It turns a simple salad into a quick, healthy, tasty weeknight meal, or serves as a little something to offer with crackers and drinks for a spontaneous get-together. I like to use a mix of chives or spring onion greens, dill, mint and flat-leaf parsley in this salad, but feel free to create your own mix of favourite herbs.

To make the herb-almond cream, stir together the sour cream, herbs, 2 tablespoons of the almonds and ⅛ teaspoon of salt in a medium bowl, then set aside.

In a small bowl, whisk together the oil, lemon juice, ¼ teaspoon of salt and a generous pinch of pepper.

Peel the cucumbers lengthways in a zebra-stripe fashion, then cut into half moons on the diagonal. Place in a large bowl together with the rocket, radishes and beetroots. Add the lemon dressing and a generous pinch of pepper, then toss to combine.

Divide the salad among 4 serving plates. Arrange the fish between the greens on the plates. Dollop with the herb-almond cream and sprinkle with the remaining almonds.

chapter six:

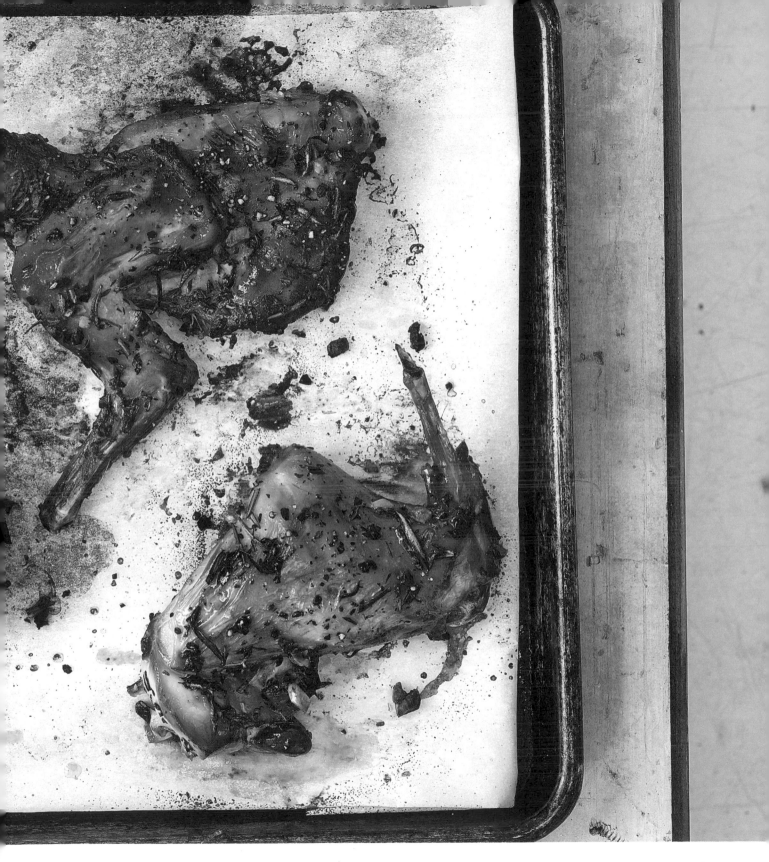

roast *charmoula* chicken, cauliflower and rocket

Charmoula is a fragrant North African sauce, typically used to flavour fish but also fantastic with chicken. I like cauliflower best when it is freshly roasted, but chicken can be roasted up to two days ahead. Allow the meat to come to room temperature before serving, if roasting ahead, and don't forget to save and gently warm the pan juices for serving.

SERVES 6

1 large head cauliflower, broken into small florets

10 tablespoons extra virgin olive oil

flaky coarse sea salt

freshly ground black pepper

2 large lemons

a handful of coriander, coarsely chopped

a small handful of flat-leaf parsley leaves, coarsely chopped

2 large garlic cloves, coarsely chopped

1 teaspoon paprika

fine sea salt

¾ teaspoon cumin

⅛ teaspoon cayenne pepper

⅛ teaspoon turmeric

1 x 1.8–2kg whole chicken

70g sultanas

115g stoned and coarsely chopped mixed olives

225g baby rocket

Place a rack in the middle of the oven and preheat to 220°C/gas mark 7. Line a baking tray with baking paper. Toss the cauliflower in a large bowl with 6 tablespoons of oil, ½ teaspoon of flaky coarse sea salt and ⅛ teaspoon of black pepper. Spread in a single layer on the baking tray and roast for 35–45 minutes, stirring occasionally, until golden and tender.

Meanwhile prepare the *charmoula*. Finely zest 1 lemon into a small bowl, then squeeze the 2 lemons to make 6 tablespoons of juice. Put the zest and 4 tablespoons of the juice into a blender (set aside the remaining juice). Add 1 tablespoon of oil, a pinch of coriander, the parsley, garlic, paprika, 1 teaspoon of fine sea salt, cumin, cayenne and turmeric. Purée until smooth.

Remove excess fat from around the cavity of the chicken, then rinse the chicken and pat dry well, inside and out. From the edge of the cavity, slip a finger under the skin of each breast, then gently but thoroughly loosen the skin from the meat of the breasts and thighs. Place the chicken into a roasting tin, breast side up, and working with about 1 tablespoon of the *charmoula* at a time, gently push 3 tablespoons into the space between the skin and flesh. As you work in the sauce, gently rub your hand over the outside of the skin to smooth out the sauce and push it further down between the skin and flesh. Reserve the remaining *charmoula*.

Quarter the lemons and stuff them into the cavity of the bird. Tie the legs together. Season with flaky coarse sea salt and pepper, brush with 1 tablespoon of oil and roast, turning once halfway through, for 45 minutes. Baste with the remaining *charmoula* and continue roasting for about 35 minutes, basting once or twice with the pan juices, until the juices of the chicken run clear when the thigh is pierced with a fork. Remove the chicken from the oven and leave to rest in the tin for 15 minutes, then transfer to a chopping board, reserving the juices. Leave to rest for 5 minutes, then carve and thickly slice.

Soak the sultanas in warm water for 10 minutes, then drain and coarsely chop. In a bowl, toss together the remaining coriander, olives and cauliflower. In another bowl, toss the rocket with the remaining 2 tablespoons of oil and 2 tablespoons of lemon juice, and a generous pinch each of flaky coarse sea salt and pepper. Mound the cauliflower mixture and rocket onto serving plates. Top with the chicken, drizzling with the pan juices.

peanut soba and chicken salad with lime

Here a zesty, crisp cabbage coleslaw meets up with rich, creamy Chinese-style cold peanut noodles. Most often I've seen this sort of noodle salad made with spaghetti or chow mein noodles, but I prefer the taste of soba – Japanese buckwheat noodles – as well as the nutrients they offer: the noodles are high in protein, fibre, iron, vitamins B[1] and B[2], the bioflavonoid rutin (a powerful antioxidant) and energy-giving complex carbs. Leftover roast pork can be used in place of the chicken, or the meat can be left out for a vegetarian option. You'll find soba noodles and chilli and garlic sauce in most large supermarkets.

SERVES 4

450g boneless chicken
  breast halves
fine sea salt
115g creamy peanut butter
4 tablespoons soy sauce
1 tablespoon rice vinegar
1 tablespoon finely chopped
  peeled ginger
1 teaspoon Chinese chilli and
  garlic sauce (see Sources,
  page 170)
1 large garlic clove, coarsely
  chopped
2 teaspoons sesame oil
2 large limes
450g Savoy cabbage, cored
  and finely shredded
8 radishes, julienned
a handful of coriander,
  coarsely chopped
2½ tablespoons grapeseed oil
340g soba noodles
3 large spring onions, julienned

Season the chicken breasts all over with ½ teaspoon of salt. Bring a large saucepan of water to a gentle simmer, then add the chicken and cook, uncovered, for 6 minutes. Remove the pan from the heat and leave to stand, covered, for about 15 minutes until the chicken is cooked through.

Meanwhile, make the peanut sauce. In a blender, combine the peanut butter, 120ml water, soy sauce, rice vinegar, ginger, chilli-garlic sauce, garlic and ¾ teaspoon of the sesame oil. Purée until smooth and set aside.

To prepare the salad, squeeze the limes to make 2½ tablespoons of juice. Cut the remaining lime into wedges and set aside. In a large bowl, toss together the cabbage, radishes, two-thirds of the coriander, lime juice, grapeseed oil, the remaining 1¼ teaspoons of sesame oil and a heaping ¼ teaspoon of salt. Toss to combine and taste and adjust the seasoning.

When the chicken is cooked, transfer it to a chopping board and leave it to cool. Bring a second large saucepan of water to the boil. Boil the noodles until just al dente, then drain and run under cold water to cool.

Drain the noodles well, transfer to a large bowl and toss with the peanut sauce. Thinly slice the chicken. Arrange the noodles in 4 large, shallow serving bowls. Top with the cabbage salad, sliced chicken, spring onions and remaining coriander. Squeeze the lime wedges over the top.

roast chicken salad with pistachio aïoli and roasted red onions

I like to serve this salad one of several ways: alongside lemon and lamb's lettuce, rocket or other peppery greens dressed with olive oil; packed into a pitta, with or without those same greens; or over toasted wholegrain bread or crackers.

SERVES 6

70g unsalted shelled pistachios
2 large red onions, sliced
    crossways into 5mm rings
4 tablespoons extra virgin
    olive oil
fine sea salt and freshly ground
    black pepper
2 garlic cloves
8 tablespoons mayonnaise
2 tablespoons fresh lemon juice
600g shredded roast chicken
    (from a 1.6–1.8kg roast or
    rotisserie chicken)
340g chicory
115g lamb's lettuce

Place a rack in the middle of the oven and preheat to 220°C/gas mark 7. Spread the pistachios on a baking tray, toast for about 5 minutes until golden and fragrant, then leave to cool completely. In a food processor, pulse all but 2 tablespoons of the pistachios until finely chopped.

Line a large rimmed baking tray with baking paper. In a large bowl, toss the onions with 2 tablespoons of the oil and season generously with salt and pepper. Spread in a single layer on the prepared baking tray and roast, stirring once, for about 25 minutes until golden brown. Remove the tray from the oven and transfer to a wire rack to allow the onions to cool.

On a chopping board, slice the garlic cloves, mound them together with a generous pinch of salt then, using both the blade and the flat side of a chef's knife, chop and scrape the mixture into a paste. Place the garlic paste, chopped pistachios, mayonnaise, 1 tablespoon of the lemon juice and 1 tablespoon of the oil in a large bowl and whisk together. Add the chicken and toss to coat. Season the chicken salad with salt and pepper.

Halve the chicory heads then cut crossways into 1cm slices. In a medium bowl, gently toss with the roasted onions, mache and the remaining tablespoon each of lemon juice and oil. Season with salt and pepper to taste. Mound the greens on 6 serving plates and top with the chicken salad. Coarsely chop the remaining 2 tablespoons of pistachios and sprinkle over the salads.

lemon-dill coleslaw and fried chicken salad

SERVES 4

For me, healthy eating is not about giving up indulgences, but rather modifying and moderating how I eat the things I love. When it comes to fried chicken, I'm happy to forgo a few of the more bulky trimmings (like gravy-drenched mashed potatoes), instead turning my crispy-battered bird into a satisfying salad with this bright, flavourful coleslaw.

180ml well-shaken buttermilk
fine sea salt and freshly ground
  black pepper
6 medium–large chicken wings
  (570g)
100g unbleached plain flour
1 teaspoon baking powder
1 teaspoon paprika
½ teaspoon dried thyme
½ teaspoon cayenne pepper
about 950ml vegetable oil
  for frying

COLESLAW
1 lemon
120ml well-shaken buttermilk
4 tablespoons finely chopped dill
2½ tablespoons Greek yogurt
  (see Box, page 84)
2 tablespoons mayonnaise
1 tablespoon extra virgin
  olive oil
½ teaspoon sugar

fine sea salt
⅛ teaspoon cayenne pepper
freshly ground black pepper
790g green cabbage, cored and
  very thinly shredded
flaky coarse sea salt

special equipment: deep-fat
  thermometer

In a large, wide bowl, whisk together the buttermilk, 2 teaspoons of fine sea salt and ⅛ teaspoon of black pepper. Add the chicken and stir to coat. Leave to stand at room temperature, stirring occasionally, for 1 hour or refrigerate for 2 hours (if refrigerating, allow the chicken to come to room temperature before frying).

In a large, shallow bowl, whisk together the flour, baking powder, 1½ teaspoons of fine sea salt, the paprika, thyme and cayenne.

Set a wire rack over a baking tray. Working with one piece at a time, remove the chicken from the buttermilk soak, allowing the excess to drip back into the bowl. Dredge the chicken in the flour mixture, pressing so it adheres to all sides. Transfer the coated chicken to the prepared rack and leave to stand at room temperature while you heat the oil.

In a deep frying pan, heat 2–3cm of oil to 180°C – check the temperature with a deep-fat thermometer. Set a second wire rack over a baking tray, or line a baking tray with kitchen paper.

Fry the chicken in batches for 5–7 minutes, turning once, until golden and cooked through, adjusting the heat as needed to maintain a temperature of around 180°C. Transfer the chicken to the wire rack or lined baking tray and leave to stand.

Meanwhile, prepare the coleslaw. Finely grate the zest from the lemon into a large bowl. Squeeze the lemon to make 1 tablespoon of juice and add it to the bowl of buttermilk together with the dill, yogurt, mayonnaise, oil, sugar, ¼ teaspoon of fine sea salt, cayenne pepper and ⅛ teaspoon of black pepper. Whisk the dressing to combine. Add the cabbage and toss well. Adjust the seasoning.

Cut the chicken wings into 2 pieces at the joints. Mound the salad on 4 serving plates. Arrange the chicken pieces on top and season the salads with black pepper and flaky coarse sea salt.

pan-seared duck salad with mango and chilli-lime vinaigrette

SERVES 4

1 x 450g magret duck breast
1½ teaspoons whole coriander
    seeds, crushed, plus more
    for garnish
fine sea salt and freshly ground
    black pepper
1 ripe mango, peeled, stoned
    and thinly sliced (see Box)
225g mizuna leaves or other
    peppery greens
4 spring onions, white and green
    parts, julienned
a handful of mixed herb leaves
    such as mint, coriander
    and basil
flaky coarse sea salt
50g coarsely chopped salted
    roasted peanuts

VINAIGRETTE

2 tablespoons finely chopped
    shallot
3 tablespoons fresh lime juice,
    plus 4 small lime wedges
    for serving
¾ teaspoon thinly sliced Thai
    or other hot chilli, plus more
    for garnish
fine sea salt
¾ teaspoon sugar
3 tablespoons grapeseed oil

The tender, crispy-skinned duck, sweet-salty combo of mango and peanuts and feisty chilli-citrus dressing brings me back to this salad again and again. Use mizuna, baby rocket or a mix with other baby greens.

Score the skin side of the duck breast in a diamond pattern. Rub the coriander seeds into the skin side, then season the duck all over with salt and pepper.

Heat a large frying pan over a medium-high heat. Place the duck, skin-side down, in the pan, reduce the heat to low and cook for 30–40 minutes, occasionally pouring off the fat, until the skin is browned and crisp.

Turn the breast skin side up and cook for a further 5 minutes for medium-rare. Transfer to a chopping board, skin side up, and leave to rest for 10 minutes.

Meanwhile, make the base for the vinaigrette. In a large mixing bowl, stir together the shallot, lime juice, chilli, ¾ teaspoon of salt and sugar. Set aside.

Thinly slice the duck breasts on a diagonal, reserving any juices from the chopping board. Arrange the mango and duck on 4 serving plates, and drizzle the duck with any juices.

To finish the vinaigrette, add the oil to the mixing bowl in a slow and steady stream, whisking vigorously. Keep whisking until the dressing is emulsified. Add the greens, spring onions and herb leaves and toss to combine. Taste and adjust the seasoning.

Mound the greens onto the plates and squeeze the lime wedges over the top. Sprinkle with the flaky coarse sea salt, peanuts, extra sliced chilli and crushed coriander seeds.

how to pick, ripen and peel a mango:

A ripe mango has a flowery scent and yields slightly when gently pressed. Under-ripe mangoes should be left at a cool room temperature for several days, or placed in a brown paper bag to speed ripening. To cut a mango, stand it on its wider end on a chopping board. Using a sharp chef's knife, cut down lengthways, along the side of the stone. Repeat on the other side, then cut away the band of fruit left around the stone. Cut the large pieces of fruit in half lengthways. Using a paring knife, cut the fruit from the skins, then slice or cube the fruit as desired.

shredded roast rabbit, sliced plum, smoked almond and shaved celery salad

This bright, crisp, nutty, meaty salad is a favourite of mine. If you're inclined after making the salad, rabbit bones make a delicious stock that can be sipped on its own or used to make a simple vegetable and noodle soup, or whatever you like (see Box below). Dark chicken meat, also nice in this salad, can be substituted for the rabbit.

SERVES 4

4 large garlic cloves, coarsely chopped
3 tablespoons coarsely chopped rosemary
3 tablespoons coarsely chopped oregano
1 rabbit (about 1.4kg), cut into 8 pieces (you can ask your butcher to prepare it for you)
6 tablespoons extra virgin olive oil, plus more for frying
fine sea salt and freshly ground black pepper
115g country bread, cut into 1cm cubes
1 celery heart (4–5 inner stalks), thinly sliced, plus celery leaves, coarsely chopped
2 plums, stoned and thinly sliced
35g smoked almonds, coarsely chopped, plus more for garnish
1 tablespoon red wine vinegar
flaky coarse sea salt

Finely chop together the garlic, rosemary and oregano. In a large bowl, toss together the rabbit, herb mixture and 3 tablespoons of the oil. Cover and leave to marinate at room temperature for 30 minutes or overnight in the fridge (if marinating overnight, bring the rabbit to room temperature before roasting).

Preheat the oven to 230°C/gas mark 8. Season the rabbit pieces all over with ¾ teaspoon of fine sea salt and ½ teaspoon of pepper. Arrange the pieces in a single layer in a baking dish, or on a rimmed baking tray lined with baking paper, and roast for about 45 minutes until golden and cooked through.

Remove the rabbit from the oven, transfer it to a chopping board and leave to rest until cool enough to handle. Cut the meat from the bones, reserving any bits of herbs and garlic. Discard the bones or use them to make a simple rabbit stock (see Box). Shred any larger pieces of meat.

Heat 1cm oil in a medium frying pan over a high heat until hot but not smoking. Add the bread cubes and fry, stirring with a slotted spoon, for about 30 seconds until golden. Drain on kitchen paper.

Place the celery heart in a large bowl. Add the shredded rabbit and the reserved herby garlic bits, the toasted bread cubes, remaining 3 tablespoons of oil, celery leaves, plums, almonds, vinegar, a few pinches of flaky coarse sea salt and pepper. Toss well to combine and adjust the seasoning to taste. Garnish with a sprinkling of the extra chopped almonds.

rabbit – a tasty, healthy, undersung protein:

Rabbit, mild and delicious, is higher in protein than beef and chicken, is rich in iron and has less fat and calories than any other meat. To make a stock with the bones, cover them with about 1.7 litres of water and add a large, coarsely chopped carrot and celery stick, a halved onion, a few sprigs of parsley and some peppercorns. Gently simmer 1–2 hours, then strain and season with fine sea salt.

za'atar roast rabbit and frisée salad with lemon vinaigrette

I like to use a mix of frisée and rocket for this lively salad, but you can stick with just one green if you prefer. Ask your butcher to prepare the rabbit.

SERVES 4

1 whole rabbit (about 1.4kg), cut into 8 pieces
2 heaped tablespoons finely chopped garlic
2 tablespoons za'atar (see Sources, page 170)
2 tablespoons extra virgin olive oil
1½ tablespoons finely chopped flat-leaf parsley
fine sea salt and coarsely ground black pepper

SALAD

2 tablespoons fresh lemon juice
1 tablespoon finely chopped shallot
fine sea salt
½ teaspoon Dijon mustard
crushed black peppercorns (see Box, page 52)
2 tablespoons good-quality extra virgin olive oil
55g frisée, torn
55g baby or wild rocket, or torn large leaves
1 medium fennel bulb, very thinly sliced

In a bowl, toss the rabbit pieces with the garlic, za'atar, oil and parsley. Cover and leave to marinate at room temperature for 30 minutes or in the fridge overnight (if marinating overnight, bring the rabbit to room temperature before roasting).

Place a rack in the middle of the oven and preheat to 230°C/gas mark 8. Line a rimmed baking tray with baking paper.

Season the rabbit with ¾ teaspoon salt and ½ teaspoon pepper. Arrange on the prepared baking tray and roast for about 45 minutes until golden and cooked through.

About 15 minutes before the end of the cooking time, prepare the salad. In a bowl, stir together the lemon juice, shallot and a scant ½ teaspoon of salt. Leave to stand for 10 minutes.

Whisk in the mustard and a generous pinch of pepper. Add the oil in a slow and steady stream, whisking vigorously. Continue to whisk until the dressing is emulsified.

Toss together the frisée, rocket and fennel in a large, wide bowl. Add the dressing and toss to combine well. Adjust the seasoning to taste.

Divide the salad among 4 serving plates and top with the warm roasted rabbit. Sprinkle with extra pepper if desired.

venison sausage with peppery greens and quick pickled peaches

The peaches make this a summer salad, but if you preserve your fruit or use shop-bought pickled peaches, you can also prepare it later in the year. Pork or chicken sausages can be substituted for the venison ones here.

SERVES 4

QUICK PICKLED PEACHES
2 medium–large firm, ripe
    peaches
½ teaspoon yellow mustard seeds
100g sugar
4 tablespoons Champagne
    vinegar
10 whole black peppercorns
5 allspice berries
1 whole clove
5cm piece of cinnamon
fine sea salt

1 tablespoon extra virgin
    olive oil
570g venison sausages
35g shelled unsalted pistachios
680g chicory
large bunch of watercress, thick
    stems trimmed
2 tablespoons extra virgin
    olive oil
2 teaspoons Champagne vinegar
fine sea salt and crushed
    black peppercorns
    (see Box, page 52)

To make the pickled peaches, cut an X in the bottom of each peach (opposite the stem end). Blanch the peaches in a medium saucepan of boiling water for 10 seconds, then drain and peel. Halve and stone the peaches, gently scraping out any rough spots where the stone was, then cut the halves into slices about 5mm thick.

Place the mustard seeds in a medium saucepan and toast over a medium heat for about 2 minutes, shaking the pan back and forth, until the seeds just start to pop. Add 240ml water and the sugar, vinegar, peppercorns, allspice, clove, cinnamon and ¼ teaspoon of salt. Bring the mixture to a simmer, stirring to dissolve the sugar. Add the peach slices and any juices. Gently simmer for 3 minutes, then remove the pan from the heat and leave the peaches to cool in the liquid for 30 minutes.

Meanwhile, heat the oil in a medium non-stick frying pan over a medium-high heat until hot but not smoking. Add the sausages, reduce the heat to medium and cook for about 10 minutes, turning frequently, until the sausages are just cooked through. Transfer to a plate.

Place the pistachios in a small frying pan and toast over a low heat for about 5 minutes, shaking the pan back and forth, until fragrant and lightly toasted. Transfer the nuts to a chopping board, leave to cool, then coarsely chop.

Cut the chicory heads crossways into 1cm slices and combine with the watercress in a large bowl. Add the oil, vinegar and a generous pinch of salt and gently toss to combine. Adjust the seasoning, then divide among 4 serving plates.

Drain the peaches and discard the spices. Slice the sausages. Arrange the peaches and sausage pieces on the serving plates and drizzle with any juices from the sausages. Sprinkle with the chopped pistachios and generous pinches of pepper.

chapter seven:

A BIT OF MEAT

beef *larb* with cabbage and green bean salad

Steve and I love exploring Queens, the huge borough to our east in New York, which is *the* place to go for Thai food. I always order the *larb* – a pungent meat-based salad and one of the most famous dishes of Laos. The best versions have a good balance of heat (from the chilli), tang (from the lime and fish sauce) and salt. Typically, toasted rice powder binds the dish and adds a nutty flavour. It's easy to make at home, but I prefer to use cashews instead. Chicken or pork can be substituted for the beef.

SERVES 4

1½ teaspoons whole coriander seeds
225g green beans, trimmed
255g green cabbage, cored and very thinly shredded
3 tablespoons coarsely chopped coriander
1½ tablespoons fish sauce
3 tablespoons fresh lime juice
1 garlic clove, finely chopped
1½ packed teaspoons brown sugar
2 tablespoons extra virgin olive oil
450g lean minced beef
fine sea salt
1 small red onion, quartered and very thinly sliced
20g very thinly sliced spring onion, whites and greens
3 tablespoons finely chopped salted roasted cashews
2 tablespoons coarsely chopped basil, plus whole leaves for garnish
3 tablespoons coarsely chopped mint
⅛ teaspoon cayenne pepper
1 medium serrano chilli, very thinly sliced

Toast the coriander seeds in a small dry frying pan over a medium-low heat for about 6 minutes, shaking the pan back and forth until fragrant. Transfer the seeds to a mini food processor or spice grinder and coarsely grind, or crush and chop using the flat side and blade of a chef's knife. Transfer to a small bowl and set aside.

Cook the green beans in a small saucepan of salted water for 1 minute. Drain and run under cold water to cool. Pat dry, then very thinly slice the beans crossways and transfer to a large bowl. Add the cabbage and 1 tablespoon of the coriander and toss to combine. Set aside.

In a small bowl, whisk together the fish sauce, 2 tablespoons of lime juice, garlic and sugar.

Heat 1 tablespoon of the oil in a large frying pan over a medium-high heat. Add the beef and ¼ teaspoon of salt and cook for about 4 minutes until cooked through, stirring with a wooden spoon and breaking up the meat. Remove the pan from the heat and add the remaining 2 tablespoons of coriander, the fish sauce mixture, the onion, spring onion, cashews, basil, mint, cayenne and half of the chilli. Stir to combine, then taste and adjust the seasoning if necessary.

Add the remaining tablespoon of lime juice to the cabbage and green beans, together with the remaining tablespoon of oil and ¼ teaspoon of salt. Toss to combine.

Divide the salad among 4 plates and top with the beef mixture. Sprinkle with the toasted coriander seeds and garnish with basil leaves and the remaining chilli.

pastrami and rye panzanella

Our dear friends, the Krutchiks, often lavish us with new food discoveries, like Wagyu pastrami – a de luxe version of the delicious brined, spiced and smoked deli meat – which they buy from their NYC neighbourhood shop, Grace's Marketplace. The richly marbled, melt-in-your-mouth meat inspired this twist on Italy's beloved bread and tomato salad. Use ripe, in-season tomatoes (their sweet juices form part of the dressing), and choose an airy, light rye bread rather than the dark, dense sort; the latter is too chewy for this salad. Wagyu is certainly tasty, but any good pastrami works well here.

SERVES 4

80g very thinly sliced red onion
155–160g cubed light rye bread
450g tomatoes, cores removed, cut into 2.5cm chunks
2 medium gherkins or 1 large European cucumber
2 celery sticks, thinly sliced
a handful of basil leaves, large leaves torn
115g sliced pastrami, coarsely chopped
a small handful of flat-leaf parsley leaves

DRESSING
1 garlic clove
fine sea salt
4 tablespoons extra virgin olive oil
1 tablespoon red wine vinegar

Place a rack in the middle of the oven and preheat the oven to 230°C/gas mark 8. Put the onion in a bowl and cover with 240–480ml of cold water. Swish the water around and rub the slices with your hands. Strain and repeat the process 2–3 times, allowing the slices to soak and changing the water at 10-minute intervals. (Soaking raw onion in cold water mellows the harsh bite.)

Meanwhile, spread out the bread cubes on a baking tray and bake for 6–8 minutes, until the edges are crispy and golden. Transfer the tray to a wire rack and leave to cool completely.

Finely chop the garlic with ¼ teaspoon salt on a chopping board. Using both the blade and the flat side of a chef's knife, chop and scrape the mixture into a paste. Put the oil and vinegar into a bowl, add the garlic paste and whisk to combine.

Combine the cooled bread cubes, the tomatoes and ¼ teaspoon of salt in a large bowl. Toss to combine, gently pressing the tomatoes to release some of the juices.

Peel the gherkins or cucumber in a zebra pattern and cut on a diagonal into half moons. Drain and pat dry the onions. Add the onions, gherkins or cucumber, celery, basil leaves, pastrami and parsley leaves to the salad. Whisk together the garlic dressing, add it to the salad and gently toss to combine.

cracked pepper *tagliata* with heirloom tomato and fresh basil salad

SERVES 4

1 tablespoons whole black
   peppercorns
1 x 450g boneless rib-eye steak,
   cut about 4cm thick, at room
   temperature
fine sea salt
1 tablespoon extra virgin
   olive oil
1 tablespoon unsalted butter

SALAD
570g mixed tomatoes
2 gherkins or 1 large cucumber
1½ tablespoons good-quality
   extra virgin olive oil
¾ teaspoon white wine vinegar
flaky coarse sea salt
a handful of torn basil leaves

Tagliata is a simple Italian preparation of good steak cooked on the rare side and thickly sliced. This version, with its thick coating of crisped cracked pepper, makes for my hands-down favourite steak salad. Best served in summer, when tomatoes are at their peak, this is one I like to present with other salads for a meal that generously serves four. For more meat, make two of these salads.

Spread the peppercorns in a single layer on a chopping board. Using the base of a Pyrex measuring jug or a small heavy-based frying pan, firmly press the peppercorns in a rocking motion to coarsely crush. Rub the peppercorns into both sides of the steak, then leave to stand at room temperature for 10 minutes.

Season the steak with ½ teaspoon of fine sea salt. Heat the oil and butter in a large cast-iron or non-stick frying pan over a high heat until the butter is melted. Add the steak and cook for 3½ minutes, then turn and cook to desired doneness – a further 3 minutes for rare. Transfer the steak to a chopping board and leave to rest for 10 minutes.

Meanwhile, prepare the salad. Halve, quarter or cut the tomatoes into 1cm wedges, depending on size. Peel the gherkins or cucumber, halve lengthwise and cut on a diagonal into half moons. Combine the tomatoes, cucumbers, good-quality olive oil and vinegar in a large bowl, and crush 1 teaspoon of flaky coarse sea salt over the top. Gently toss together to combine, then add the basil and toss once more. Adjust the seasoning to taste.

Divide the salad among 4 serving plates. Surround each salad with slices of steak.

lamb *fattoush*

SERVES 4

450g boneless lamb chump
    roast
7g finely chopped mint, plus
    a handful of coarsely
    chopped mint
1 tablespoon extra virgin
    olive oil
115g sugar-snap peas, strings
    removed
2 cos lettuce hearts, torn
450g tomatoes, cut into
    1cm wedges
1 large cucumber, peeled and
    cut crossways into 5mm pieces
4 large radishes, thinly sliced
3 spring onions (whites and
    greens), very thinly sliced
125g feta cheese, crumbled
sumac, optional (see Sources,
    page 170)

DRESSING
1 large garlic clove, finely
    chopped, plus 1 large clove
    left whole
fine sea salt and freshly ground
    black pepper
3½ tablespoons good-quality
    extra virgin olive oil
2½ tablespoons fresh lemon
    juice
⅛ teaspoon cayenne pepper

A vibrant, beloved bread and vegetable Lebanese salad, *fattoush* is dressed with a robust garlic and lemon juice vinaigrette and seasoned with sumac, a pleasingly astringent spice made from the ground dried berries of the sumac tree. Here I've added a bit of lamb rubbed with garlic and mint: not classic but tasty, and the meat can be left out for a vegetarian version.

Place a rack in the middle of the oven and preheat to 220°C/gas mark 7.

In a baking dish, rub the lamb with the mint, 1 tablespoon of oil, the chopped garlic, ½ teaspoon of salt and ⅛ teaspoon of pepper. Roast for 16–18 minutes, or until a meat thermometer inserted in the centre reads 57°C for medium-rare. Transfer the lamb to a chopping board and leave to rest for 10 minutes, then slice and set aside.

Cook the peas in a small pan of salted boiling water for 1½ minutes, then drain and cool under cold running water.

To make the vinaigrette, slice the garlic on a chopping board using a chef's knife, then mound together with ½ teaspoon of salt. Using both the blade and the flat side of the knife, chop and scrape the mixture into a paste. Whisk together the garlic paste and lemon juice in a large, wide bowl, then whisk in the good-quality oil and cayenne pepper.

Place the lettuce, tomatoes, cucumber and radish in the bowl with the vinaigrette and add the sugar snap peas, spring onions and coarsely chopped mint. Toss to combine well, then crumble the feta on top and sprinkle with sumac to taste if using.

Mound the salad onto 4 serving plates and surround each salad with slices of lamb.

spicy lamb brochettes over a green bean, sugar snap pea and grilled onion salad

A lemony yogurt dressing forms the base of this pretty salad. I like to cut the green beans in half lengthways, which is attractive and makes for a more delicate bite. But this extra step isn't a must, and can be skipped if you prefer not to fuss.

SERVES 4

570g boneless leg of lamb or
    lamb shoulder, cut into
    2.5cm cubes
2 garlic cloves, very thinly sliced
¾ teaspoon piment d'Espelette
    or ¼ teaspoon cayenne pepper
225g green beans, trimmed and
    cut in half lengthways
225g sugar-snap peas, strings
    removed
2 small red onions
5 tablespoons extra virgin
    olive oil
a handful plus 1 tablespoon
    coarsely chopped mint

DRESSING
1 lemon
75ml Greek yogurt (see Box,
    page 84)
flaky coarse sea salt and freshly
    ground black pepper

Special Equipment:
metal or wooden skewers

Finely grate the zest of the lemon into a large bowl, reserving the fruit. Add the lamb, garlic and piment d'Espelette, then cover and marinate at room temperature for 1 hour or in the fridge overnight. (If marinating overnight, bring the meat to room temperature before grilling.) If using wooden skewers, soak in water for 10 minutes.

Bring a medium saucepan of boiling salted water to the boil. Add the green beans and sugar-snap peas, and cook for about 1½ minutes until just until crisp-tender. Drain, place in a large bowl and set aside.

Squeeze the reserved lemon to make 2 teaspoons of juice, then pour into a small bowl. Add the yogurt and a generous pinch each of salt and pepper, stir together and set aside.

Preheat the grill to medium-high.

Cut the onions into 1cm wedges, keeping the root end intact. Toss with 1½ tablespoons of oil and season generously with salt and pepper. Grill, turning occasionally, until golden and tender, about 5 minutes for medium-rare. Transfer to a plate to cool slightly.

Toss the lamb with 1 tablespoon of oil and season generously with salt and pepper. Thread the lamb pieces onto the skewers and grill for 3–4 minutes, turning occasionally, until cooked to medium-rare. Transfer to a chopping board and leave to rest for 5 minutes.

Meanwhile, add the onion wedges, mint, remaining 2½ tablespoons of oil and a generous pinch each of salt and pepper to the bowl with the green bean mixture. Gently toss together, then taste and adjust the seasoning.

Spoon the yogurt mixture onto 4 serving plates and top with the bean salad and skewers.

vitello tonnato and crisped celery salad

SERVES 4

VITELLO TONNATO
1 medium onion, halved
  and peeled
1 carrot, cut crossways into
  3 pieces
1 celery stick, cut crossways
  into 3 pieces
4 leafy sprigs of parsley
1 leafy sprig each of sage and
  rosemary (optional)
1 bay leaf
½ teaspoon whole
  peppercorns
450–680g veal loin or pork
  tenderloin
1½ tablespoons capers,
  preferably salt-packed
  (see Box, page 32)
140g tuna in olive oil,
  drained
2 medium egg yolks
3 oil-packed anchovy fillets
½ teaspoon Dijon mustard
fine sea salt
1 lemon
8 tablespoons extra virgin
  olive oil

CELERY SALAD
4 celery stalks from the inner
  heart, plus celery leaves
2 tablespoons extra virgin
  olive oil
flaky coarse sea salt
coarsely cracked black
  pepper

One of Italy's most famous cold meat dishes, *vitello tonnato* (chilled veal in a tuna sauce) makes a gorgeous salad plate, especially with elegant curls of shaved celery. If you have time, make the dish one day ahead, layering spoonfuls of sauce between the slices of meat, then refrigerate, covered; the flavours will significantly deepen as they macerate. Pork loin or turkey can also be used here instead of veal.

In a medium saucepan, combine the onion, carrot, celery, parsley, sage and rosemary (if using), bay leaf and peppercorns. Add 1.4 litres of water, bring to a simmer, then add the veal (the water should just cover the vegetables and meat – add more water if necessary). Return to a simmer, then reduce the heat as necessary to cook, covered, at a gentle simmer for 35–50 minutes, until a meat thermometer inserted diagonally into the meat reads 65°C. Remove the pan from the heat and leave the veal to cool completely in the stock.

Rinse and soak the capers in cold water for 10 minutes. Rinse again and pat dry, then place into a food processor and combine with the tuna, egg yolks, anchovies, mustard and ¼ teaspoon of fine sea salt. Finely grate the zest of the lemon into the bowl, holding the lemon close to the bowl to capture the flavourful oil. Squeeze the lemon to make 1½ tablespoons of juice. Add to the bowl, then, with the machine running, add the oil, a few drops at a time, in a slow and steady stream.

Slice the meat and fan out on the plates, adding spoonfuls of the *tonnato* sauce between the meat slices.

To make the celery salad, trim and cut the celery stalks crossways in half. Using a mandoline, carefully shave the pieces, starting with the base of the U shape of the celery facing down (if you don't have a mandoline, cut the celery into thin julienne strips). Submerge the shaved celery in a large bowl of iced water and leave to stand for 30 minutes.

Drain the celery and gently pat dry with kitchen paper. In a large, dry bowl, toss the celery with the oil. Season generously with flaky coarse sea salt and black pepper. Divide the salad among 4 large serving plates. Sprinkle with the celery leaves and more black pepper.

frisée and cucumber salad with mexican-spiced pork and guacamole

SERVES 4

450g pork cutlets
3 garlic cloves, finely chopped
3 tablespoons fresh orange juice
1 ¼ teaspoons chilli powder
fine sea salt and freshly ground
   black pepper
2 tablespoons extra virgin
   olive oil

GUACAMOLE
2 large jalepeño chiles
2 firm, ripe avocados, stoned
   and cut into 5mm cubes (see
   Box)
4 tablespoons fresh lime juice
6 tablespoons finely chopped red
   or white onion
a small handful, plus
   2 tablespoons coarsely
   chopped coriander
fine sea salt

SALAD
225g frisée
1 gherkin
10g whole coriander leaves
35ml good-quality extra virgin
   olive oil
20ml white balsamic vinegar
flaky coarse sea salt

My cousin Katharine's fantastic signature guacamole – a perfectly balanced mix of creamy chunks of avocado, coarsely chopped jalapeños, fresh lime juice and fine sea salt (gently stirred, not mashed) – single-handedly inspired this salad.

Place the pork cutlets, garlic, orange juice and chilli powder in a bowl, and toss together to combine well. Leave to marinate at room temperature for 30 minutes or in the fridge overnight (if marinating overnight, bring the pork to room temperature before roasting).

Season the pork all over with ¾ teaspoon of salt and ¼ teaspoon of pepper. Heat the oil in a large non-stick or cast-iron frying pan over a medium-high heat until hot but not smoking. Add the cutlets and cook for about 7 minutes, turning once halfway through, until the meat is cooked but slightly pink in the centre. Transfer to a chopping board and leave to rest.

To make the guacamole, seed and coarsely chop the jalapeños, reserving the seeds depending on your taste for heat. Combine in a medium bowl with the avocado, lime juice, onion, coriander and ½ teaspoon of salt. Gently stir to combine (do not mash).

To prepare the salad, tear the frisée and thinly slice the gherkin into rounds, then toss with the coriander leaves in a large bowl. Add the oil and vinegar, sprinkle with ½ teaspoon of flaky sea salt and toss to combine well.

Slice the pork. Mound the salad onto 4 serving plates. Surround each salad with slices of pork and spoonfuls of guacamole.

choosing a good avocado:

Avocados can be a bit deceiving; even unblemished ones that feel heavy for their size and yield slightly to pressure (all good ripeness indicators) can sometimes taste bland. A gentle press should cause the fruit to yield slightly or produce a small dent. A large dent points to an overripe avocado, which will render a blackened, bitter-tasting flesh. A hard avocado can be ripened on the work surface for 3–6 days, or more rapidly in a brown paper bag with an apple or banana inside.

spicy cabbage, celery and pickled jalapeño coleslaw with sweet barbecue-style ribs

SERVES 4

RIBS

2 spring onions, coarsely
  chopped
2 large garlic cloves, coarsely
  chopped
4 teaspoons chilli powder
2½ teaspoons dried oregano,
  crumbled (see Box, page 61)
1½ teaspoons paprika,
  preferably smoked (see
  Sources, page 170)
fine sea salt
¼ teaspoon cayenne pepper
1 x 8-rib rack pork spare ribs
  (about 900g)
360ml dark ale
120ml good-quality bottled
  barbecue sauce

COLESLAW

2 large jalapeño peppers
6 tablespoons distilled
  white vinegar
4 teaspoons sugar
1 large garlic clove, thinly sliced
¼ teaspoon dried thyme
570g red cabbage
4 celery stalks, from the inner
  heart, plus leaves
2 tablespoons extra virgin oil
2 tablespoons red wine vinegar
fine sea salt

Barbecue dishes are often considered to be summer food, but Steve and I like to indulge in this salad all year long. The ribs are baked in the oven, during which time you can prepare a quick, tasty jalapeño-and-garlic pickle that makes this coleslaw a standout. I serve two ribs per person for this salad, but you can prepare the ribs as main-course fare by simply doubling or tripling the recipe, depending on your crowd.

Place a rack in the middle of the oven and preheat to 200°C/gas mark 6.

To make the ribs, combine the spring onions, garlic, chilli powder, oregano, paprika, ½ teaspoon of salt and cayenne pepper in the bowl of a food processor and process to a paste.

Score the fat side of the ribs, place in a large roasting tin and rub all over with the spice paste. Pour the beer around the ribs. Cover the pan tightly with foil and bake for about 1½ hours, until the ribs are tender and falling off the bone.

To make the coleslaw, thinly slice the jalapeños crossways, reserving the seeds. In a very small frying pan, combine the vinegar and sugar. Bring the mixture to the boil, whisking to dissolve the sugar. Add the jalapeños with seeds and the garlic, reduce the liquid to a simmer and cook, gently stirring, for 30 seconds, then stir in the thyme. Transfer the mixture to a heatproof bowl and leave to cool completely for about 20 minutes.

Meanwhile, core and thinly slice the red cabbage. Very thinly slice the celery stalks and leaves. Combine all three in a large bowl.

Remove the ribs from the oven, leave them to rest for 10 minutes, then cut them into individual ribs. Warm the barbecue sauce, then brush the ribs with the sauce.

Finish the coleslaw by adding the pickled jalapeño and garlic mixture, with its pickling liquid, to the cabbage and celery, then add the oil, vinegar and ½ teaspoon of salt. Toss to combine well. Divide the coleslaw among 4 serving plates and top with the ribs.

Roman spiced pork loin and rocket salad with roasted grapes and marcona almonds

Seasoning a pork loin with garlic, rosemary and fennel and roasting it in a bundle of bacon gives this salad a few flavour cues from one of my favourite Roman pork preparations, *porchetta*. The pork can be roasted up to three days ahead; its flavour will intensify and it's great served cold or at room temperature. I use a mixture of rocket and frisée lettuce here; the duo lends a nice texture and a pleasing balance of peppery bitterness but you can choose to use all of one type if you prefer.

SERVES 4

PORK
1½ teaspoons fennel seed
2 large garlic cloves
fine sea salt and freshly ground
  black pepper
1 tablespoon finely chopped
  rosemary
1 teaspoon extra virgin olive oil
450–570g pork tenderloin
150g sliced bacon

SALAD
1 teaspoon black peppercorns
450g grapes, seedless red,
  green, black or a mix
6 rosemary leaves
70g sugar
fine sea salt
1½ tablespoons red wine vinegar
2 teaspoons finely chopped
  shallot
½ teaspoon finely chopped garlic

2 tablespoons extra virgin
  olive oil
freshly ground black pepper
140g baby or wild rocket,
  or torn large leaves
115g frisée, torn
70g Marcona almonds, or
  salted roasted peanuts,
  coarsely chopped
flaky coarse sea salt

Place a rack in the middle of the oven and preheat to 160°C/gas mark 3.

Make the pork: Using a spice grinder, pestle and mortar or chef's knife, coarsely grind or chop the fennel seeds. Slice the garlic with a chef's knife on a chopping board, then mound together with ½ teaspoon of salt and ¼ teaspoon of pepper. Using both the blade and the flat side of the knife, chop and scrape the mixture into a paste. Transfer the paste to a small bowl, add the oil, rosemary and fennel, and stir.

With a paring knife, make 12 X-shaped incisions, about 3mm deep, all over the pork and stuff with a quarter of the herb mixture. Rub the outside of the loin with the rest of the mixture. Starting at one end of the loin, wrap the pork in bacon (do not overlap the bacon slices). Place the pork in a baking dish or gratin and roast for 30 minutes. Baste the pork with its juices and continue roasting for about 10 minutes, until a meat thermometer inserted in the centre reads 60°C. Transfer the pork to a chopping board and leave to rest while you prepare the salad.

Reduce the oven temperature to 130°C/gas mark 1.

Spread the peppercorns in a single layer on a chopping board. Using the base of a Pyrex measuring jug or a small heavy-based frying pan, firmly press the peppercorns in a rocking motion to coarsely crush. Put the peppercorns, grapes and rosemary leaves in a large heatproof bowl set on a wire rack.

In a small saucepan, combine the sugar, ¼ teaspoon of fine sea salt and 75ml water. Bring the mixture to the boil, then remove from the heat and whisk until the sugar is mostly dissolved. Pour the simple syrup over the grape mixture and gently stir once to combine. Leave to stand for 10 minutes, then strain and transfer the grapes to a rimmed baking tray. Roast for about 30 minutes until the grapes are tender and the skins are slightly wrinkled and tacky. Transfer the pan to a wire rack to cool while you finish the salad.

In a small bowl, mix together the vinegar, shallot, garlic, ¾ teaspoon of fine sea salt and ⅛ teaspoon pepper. Whisk in the oil. Add the rocket and frisée, then add the dressing and toss to combine well. Adjust the seasoning to taste.

Slice the pork. Divide the salad and pork among 4 serving plates. Sprinkle with the grapes and almonds and crush a little flaky coarse sea salt over the top.

Sources and Credits

ANCHOVIES
White anchovies are sold both packaged and loose by weight. Look for them at the deli counter of the supermarket or in Italian and Spanish speciality shops.

BOOKS
Among my favourite resources about sea salt and about choosing and using fruits and vegetables are: *Salted* by Mark Bitterman (see more under Salt, page 10) and *Chez Panisse Fruit* and *Chez Panisse Vegetables*, both by Alice Waters (all three also include terrific recipes); and *Wellness Foods A to Z*, by Sheldon Margen, MD, a comprehensive and interesting nutrition-focused resource that includes ingredient tips and more.

ASIAN PRODUCTS
Chilli garlic sauce, Sriracha, fish sauce, fresh ginger and other Asian groceries can be found in the Asian sections at most good supermarkets.

CAPERS
Salt-packed capers are available at specialty shops, and in Waitrose and at www.ocado.com and Brindisa (The Floral Hall, Stoney Street, Borough Market, London SE1 9AF; 020-7407-1036; brindisa.com).

CHORIZO AND MORCILLA SAUSAGES
Brindisa (see above) is also a great source for chorizo and morcilla sausages, as well as Spanish olive oils, vinegars, rice, Pimentón de la Vera (smoked paprika), pimento peppers, olives and other hand-selected products from Spain.

DRIED BEANS, GRAINS AND LEGUMES
For Colfiorito lentils from Umbria, go to guidetti.co.uk. Look for French green lentils at fine supermarkets, like Whole Foods Market, wholefoodsmarket.com. Spanish pardina lentils can be ordered from The Tapas Lunch Company (408 Broome Street, New York, NY 10013; 212-219-5050; despananyc.com).

At Whole Foods Market, wholefoodsmarket.com, you can purchase fantastic dried heirloom beans by mail order. Giganti beans can be mail ordered from Kalustyan's (kalustyans.com). Good quality dried beans can also be purchased from a reputable grocer and use by 'best by date. Farro can be purchased at Whole Foods Market, wholefoodsmarket. com; Luigi's Delicatessen (luigismailorder.com); and Guidetti Fine Foods (guidetti. co.uk; 020-7635-9800), which also stocks a great selection of cheeses, olive oils, cured meats, spices and more.

Freekeh can be found at Whole Foods Market, or ordered from Melbury and Appleton Delicatessen and Grocer (0843-289-1880; melburyandappleton. co.uk).

HERBS
Dried Greek oregano and other high-quality Greek products, can be purchased at Eleon Foods (eleonfinefoods.co.uk)

HONEY
Chestnut honey and other fine honeys can be purchased at fine cheese shops or Melbury and Appleton Delicatessen and Grocer (0843-289-1880; melburyandappleton.co.uk).

NUTS
Purchase Marcona almonds at Whole Foods Market, wholefoodsmarket.com and Natoora (020-7627-1600; natoora.co.uk), or fine grocers and cheese shops.

OLIVE OILS AND OTHER OILS
For a terrific selection of estate-bottled extra-virgin olive oils from Italy, look to Luigi's (luigismailorder.com). Fantastic

Spanish olive oils, including Castillo de Canena, can be found at Brindisa (The Floral Hall, Stoney Street, Borough Market, London SE1 9AF; 020-7407-1036; brindisa.com). Find other fine estate-bottled extra-virgin olive oils at Melbury and Appleton Delicatessen and Grocer (0843-289-1880; melburyandappleton.co.uk).

O Olive Oil makes great citrus oils. Look for them at oilandmore.co.uk and Whole Foods Market, wholefoodsmarket.com

Look for cold-pressed pumpkin-seed oil at natoora.com and amazon.com. Squash-seed oil can be found at wholeheartedfoods.com.

PASTA
Good quality pastas can be purchased at Whole Foods Market and other good supermarkets. One of my favorite brands, Pasta Setaro, as well as whole-wheat pastas and high-quality farro, can be found at Sud Ovest (54 Coombe Road, Kingston-upon-Thames, Surrey, KT2 7AF; 020-8549-0084; sudovest.co.uk).

POTS, PANS AND TOOLS
I highly recommend Le Creuset enameled cast-iron gratin dishes, grill pans and Dutch ovens (lecreuset.com).

Berndes makes fantastic nonstick pans. I like the 'Tradition' line, which is made using vacuum-pressured casting. They heat evenly, the coating does not chip,

and with the handles wrapped in foil, they can be used in the oven. Find them at amazon.com.

Shop Lodge (lodgemfg.com) for cast-iron pans.

Joyce Chen Scissors are invaluable for snipping herbs, cutting through cooked lobster shells, cutting the backbone out of a chicken and more. Look for them at amazon.com and chefscatalog.com.

Benringer adjustable-blade slicers can be found at Chinatown shops and at Richmond Cookshop (01202 749428; richmondcookshop.co.uk).

SEA SALT
A wide array of exceptional fine, medium and coarse flaky sea salts, for basic cooking, finishing and special seasoning, can be purchased at justingredients.co.uk. One of my go-to everyday salts is Big Tree Farms (Coarse Hollow Pyramids and a fine grain Fleur de Sel); find both at amazon.com.

Mark Bitterman's book, *Salted: A Manifesto on the World's Most Essential Mineral* turned me into a complete salt nut, and is a tome I reach for often for information and recipes. The book includes a field guide to artisan salts and a quick-reference guide, covering over 150 salts, as well as fascinating information on the nutritional value and production of salt.

SPICES
Aleppo pepper, Piment d'espelette, Pimentón de la Vera (Spanish smoked paprika), sumac, za'atar, wonderfully aromatic black, white and red peppercorns and other high-quality spices and food products can be purchased at The Spice Shop (1 Blenheim Crescent, W11 2EE London; 020-7221-4448; thespiceshop.co.uk).

VINEGARS
Delizia Estense makes two agrodolce vinegars – a white wine and a red wine version – that are a staple in my pantry and make fantastic gifts. They can be purchased from Delizia Estense (deliziaestense.it). Look for other great vinegars at Melbury and Appleton Delicatessen and Grocer (0843-289-1880; melburyandappleton.co.uk) and other good cheese shops.

BEAUTIFUL OBJECTS IN THIS BOOK
Many of the gorgeous props that appear in the pages of this book were generously donated by ABC Carpet & Home, www.abchome.com; 212-473-3000.

Index

Acknowledgements

Loads of good energy, time, effort, critical thinking and creative muscle from many talented people went into the making of this book. I am deeply appreciative.

Thank you to my Kyle Books team: my amazing editor Anja Schmidt, who offered her invaluable resourcefulness, organisation, creativity, spirit and support at every stage of this project; Kyle Cathie, for including me in an exciting family of wonderful authors; Sarah Scheffel, for meticulous copy editing, and thoughtful and fantastic suggestions; and Ron Longe, for terrific support, reach and zeal.

Enormous thanks to my visual dream team, whose talent, intuition, innovation and dedication brought a sumptuous simple elegance to these pages: photographer Ellen Silverman, prop stylist Lucy Attwater, food stylist Rebecca Jurkevich and designer Carl Hodson, and to production managers Gemma John and Nic Jones. Huge thanks, as well, to our crew of energetic and detailed photography, and food and prop styling assistants: Kevin Norris, Nidia Cueva, Sam Napolitano, Artemis Millan, Molly Shuster and Tina DeGraff; and to ABC Carpet & Home, for loaning heaps of exquisite props.

To my agent, David Black: thank you for your boundless support and attention, thoughtful opinions and ideas, and keen matchmaking skills. And to your attentive and organized staff, Allie Hemphill and Gary Morris; it is a real pleasure to work with you all.

To my stalwart and generous recipe testers, Linsey Herman and Cameron Kane, and my spirited and savvy assistant, Sue Li: your keen palates and ideas are reflected in so many pages of this book.

The exceptional feedback and support that I receive from friends and colleagues – talented creatives in this field and others – is invaluable. Thank you to Jennifer Aaronson, Lisa Amand, Jeanne Atkin, Tanya and Alf Bishai, Tom Castele, Karen DeMasco, Sam Douglas, Curt Feldman, Stefan Forbes, G. Giraldo, David and Butch Krutchik, Gabrielle Langholtz, Robin Insley, Irene Hamburger, Marisa Huff, Emma and Mitchell Hulse, Bill Hutchinson, Sara Jenkins, John Kim, Alison Tozzi Liu, Sioux Logan, Julie Miller, Sarah Ann Mockbee, Paul Molakides, Jocelyn Morse-Farmerie, Katharine Page and Mark von Holstein, Raquel Pelzel, Corina Quinn, Alex Raij, Amie Rogosin Ruditz, Dave Sanford, Gail Simmons, Jon and Michelle Tate, Meeghan Truelove, John Wasiniak, Michael Wilson, Tia Wou and Amy Zavatto, as well as families Abrams, Brown, Costello, Hoffman, Kaminsky, Levitt, Mockbee, Rudley, Sambursky, Schiffman, Simmons and Steinmetz.

Thank you to Denise Lauffer for exceptional pup care and extra walks – a significant contribution to this book and other projects.

Endless gratitude to my parents, Neil and Phyllis Fox, for fostering my vision of the world through the food lens and passing on your talents in the kitchen, and to my brother, Jason Fox, a talented chef and forager: I so enjoy and am continuously energised by sharing time at the stove with you all.

To my little black hound dog, Jasper Lee: 48 pounds of love and devotion, and the perfect kitchen and writing companion.

And to my husband and best friend, Steve Hoffman: our adventures together in food and life provide immeasurable inspiration and happiness.

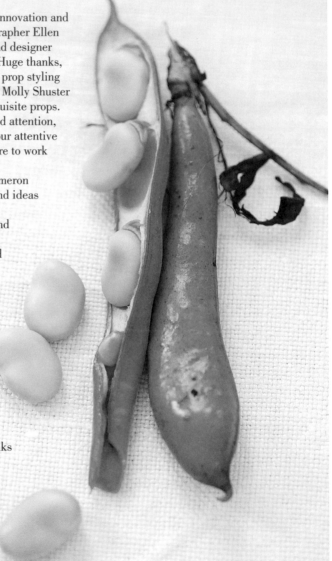